THE PERFECT WEEK FORMULA

CONTENTS

INTRODUCTION: YOUR PERFECT WEEK

Dateline: Wednesday, 4:59 pm.
Location: Chino Hills, CA

I was in the passenger seat of a black SUV.

My driver, a big old Armenian that looked like a Barbarian at the gates of Rome, was driving us home from the headquarters of his fitness franchise Fit Body Boot Camp.

His name is Bedros Keuilian, and, in addition to being my business partner, he's also been one of my closest friends for over a decade.

As we barrelled down the highway, Bedros and I talked endlessly about business strategy, leadership, and the entrepreneurial lifestyle.

We joked, laughed, and seemed to be having a great time...

...Until we arrived at our destination.

Bedros turned to me, unlocked the car, flashed me his "Armenian Death Stare", and said in a gruff tone, "You're on your own, buddy."

I jumped out of the car, and took my backpack up to his guest house where I was spending the night. I wouldn't see him again until morning.
To the outside observer, this interaction probably doesn't make sense.

It wasn't like I said something to offend him when we rolled down his driveway.

But when you understand the context of his statement, the picture becomes clear.

Several years ago, Bedros made a *non-negotiable* commitment to his wife that Wednesday nights at 5 pm was the official start of date night. And, not only has he made that promise to *her* but he lets everyone on his team and in his inner circle know that this time is for him, his wife...and no one else (not even 'Ol Craiggy, his brother from another mother from Canadia, as he calls it).

And it's this commitment to his personal non-negotiables that is responsible for the success he enjoys today.

Unlike most entrepreneurs (even hyper-successful ones), Bedros has it all. He has an amazing relationship with his wife and children, all-day energy, a thriving business, and a deeply fulfilling personal life.

All because he has committed to *building his business around his life, not his life around his business.*

But he wasn't always like this.

Only a few years ago, Bedros was struggling. He couldn't seem to crack the code to making his life work.

Sure, he could make a ton of money. But it came at the expense of his family and health.

And if he shifted gears, prioritizing his family and fitness, his business would suffer and the empire he'd built would crumble around him.

No matter what he did or how hard he tried to "hustle" his way out of his problems, nothing seemed to work. One day, it all came to a head when he suffered (much like I did nearly ten years earlier) from an anxiety attack that was *so* bad he thought he was going to die.

In his book *Man Up,* he shares how my coaching helped him overcome his anxiety and fix the problems facing him in his life and business. It wasn't easy. But little by little, with the help of his family and network, Bedros turned everything around and became the unstoppable leader he is today.

Throughout this book, I'm going to teach you the exact same strategies and tactics that helped Bedros transform from a struggling, anxious, and burned out entrepreneur into the high-performing Empire Builder the world is blessed to have today.

But first, I need to make a confession.

In the summer of 2018, three years after I wrote my first best-selling book *The Perfect Day Formula*--a step-by-step guide to conquering the chaos of your days and achieving peak performance--I came to a startling realization.

I had written the wrong book...

Don't get me wrong... *The Perfect Day Formula* was a game changer and it's helped tens of thousands of entrepreneurs work less, earn more, and live better lives.

But every day when I open my inbox or read one of the hundreds of book reviews, I was greeted with new questions about the system:

"How does this work if you have kids?"

"How does this apply to the weekends?"

"Do I have to get up at 4 o'clock in the morning?"

"What if my work life is different every day of the week?"

The Perfect Day Formula gave my readers an effective, but incomplete system for work life mastery and left many questions unanswered.

So, over the past year, I've set out to remedy the situation.

After pouring over dozens of questions from my top clients and spending 75 full-day coaching sessions developing and testing a new system, I wrote the book that I *should* have written in the first place...

The Perfect Week Formula.

Before we can work together to help you engineer your perfect weeks (and, as a result, your perfect *life*), you must first have a clear picture of what these weeks will look like.

Remember: *Before something can be achieved, it must first be defined.*

So right now, I want you to imagine your perfect week.

Picture a week where everything goes according to plan. Where you sit down each day with laser like focus, speeding through your most important tasks, making massive progress on what matters, and finishing the work day with more free time than you've ever had before.

A week where you are able to grow your business or advance your career without sacrificing your *life* instead of trying to fit in a little life around your working hours.

What would you do differently in your Perfect Week than you do today?

Would you finally make date night a real priority? Take your kids for an unforgettable backpacking trip? Get back into the gym on a consistent basis? Carve out more time to read great books, play your favorite instrument, or learn a new language?

Picture this week now.

The idea of bridging the gap between how you are living *today* and how you want to live in the future can feel overwhelming at first. In some cases, it might even seem impossible.

When you look at the never-ending list of to-do's staring at you each morning, you might think to yourself, "I could never have a perfect week that looks like that. I have way too much to do."

But I promise, you can.

You just need the right system to make it happen.

And in this book I'm giving you that system. A roadmap used by hundreds of my most successful clients that allowed them to earn more, work less, and live the life they always wanted.

What you're about to learn is simple, so simple you might be skeptical it could work for anyone, let alone for you.

But work it does. This simple plan has worked for me, it's worked for my clients, and it's worked for thousands of people who read my content every single week.

You're about to get the exact formula that I've personally used over the past decade to build five 7-figure businesses, coach 8 and 9-figure entrepreneurs across dozens of industries, write multiple books (including a Wall Street Journal Best-Seller), spend hours every day with my wife and family, travel the world, and live my perfect life.

By the end of the book you'll be familiar with success terms like "Golden Handcuffs", "NN", "NUI Work", "Magic Time", the "Reverse Alarm", and the "7x7 Grid"

But for now, simply trust the process.

Trust that, if you put in the work and learn from people who have "been there, done that" you *can* have it all.

This formula has worked for all of my top clients and it will work for you too.

My client Isabel Price used these lessons to grow her nutrition coaching company to more than 8-figures in yearly revenue while still making time for her family and social life. Today, she works from 9 am until 2 pm, home schools both of her children, goes on weekly date nights, and still makes time for regular workouts and self care.

Another client I've worked with, a young man named Jason Capital, used my coaching to build a $10 million/ year business before the age of 30 while travelling the world, staying at 5-star hotels, enjoying the finer things in life, and still making time for his girlfriend, workouts, and mentoring millions of young entrepreneurs around the globe.

This system also helped my friend, business partner, and coaching client Bedros Keuilian overcome his entrepreneurial anxiety, increase his income, and create the structure he needed to turn his floundering business into one of the fastest growing franchises in America.

Like all of my best clients--and like you--Isabel, Jason, and Bedros were already high-performers when I started working with them and I won't try to take credit for their results.

I didn't do the work for them. I simply provided them with the direction and structure they needed to get to the next level.

They were the ones who did the hard work and found the treasure map for their success. I was just the mentor that came along and gave them a few tools to achieve it faster.

What I gave them is the same thing I'm offering you today. A blueprint to reclaim control of your time and your life. A proven system to "have it all" and achieve your biggest goals without sacrificing the things that matter most.

A formula for your perfect week.

Put in the work and I promise you, *The Perfect Week Formula* will change your life in ways you can't imagine.

I look forward to hearing about your success.

Sincerely,

Craig Ballantyne
Craig@PerfectWeekFormula.com

ONE

PRISON BREAK: HOW TO ESCAPE THE GOLDEN HANDCUFFS AND GET CONTROL OF YOUR LIFE

When I was a young(er) man, nearly two decades ago, my life was in a rut.

I was a broke, struggling, binge drinking, socially anxious personal trainer...who had *zero* desire to be a broke, struggling, binge drinking, socially anxious personal trainer.

It wasn't that I hated my clients or disliked the work.

I just didn't want to be someone else's rep-counting towel boy. I was tired of braving minus 20 degree temperatures to catch the 5am bus downtown to make it to my first appointment. And I was fed up with working split shifts that kept me away from home for 14 hours a day.

But most of all, I hated feeling trapped.

I hated being chained to a job that I didn't like so that I could make just enough money to fund my weekend drinking habit and then wake up to drag my butt and anxious brain out of bed on Monday morning to do it all over again.

I wanted the freedom that came with being an entrepreneur, but I had no idea how to get started.

Eventually, I decided enough was enough.

I was done with the 9-5 grind (or in my case, the 6-7 grind) and was going to do whatever it took to earn my freedom.

Over the months that followed, I set about devouring every book, video, and course I could get my hands on. And somewhere along the line I stumbled across a mentor named Michael Masterson, the founder of EarlyToRise. com, who taught me several foundational pillars of *The Perfect Week Formula* (even though I didn't know it at the time), including:

Prioritizing non-urgent but important work.

It wasn't "urgent" to work on my side business. I wouldn't lose my job and my girlfriend wouldn't dump me if I decided not to do it. (In fact both of those would benefit if I skipped it.)

But I wanted freedom and was willing to do whatever it took to get it.

That's when I started waking up 15 minutes earlier each day and investing the first 15 minutes of my mornings into making my dream a reality.

Success didn't happen overnight. But little by little, day by day, I started to make progress. And within 18 months, I had built a thriving 6-figure online business, quit my job as a personal trainer, and achieved the freedom I'd been after for so long...

...Sort of.

After making my escape, I quickly became addicted to my newfound success and, within a year, my life was, once again, out of control. Twelve hour days became the 'norm'. I shut out my friends and family to focus on growing my empire. Goodbye girlfriend, hello grind. I started working weekends, skipping social events, and rolled my eyes when my family and friends told me to take a vacation.

For years, I struggled to find time for myself. My life was built around my businesses and I believed the lie most high-performers tell themselves that, "This is just how it is." And even when I didn't have work to do, I lacked the ability to do anything else, and so I found some work-related tasks to fill the void.

There was no end in sight and whenever my friends or family tried to tell me (as gently as possible) that I'd become a full blown workaholic, I would say to myself, "They just don't get it! They have no idea how busy I am."

As the old saying goes, I was so busy making a living that I forgot to make a life.

It took two trips to the emergency room and nearly six month of ongoing anxiety attacks (detailed in my WSJ bestseller *Unstoppable*) for me to wake up to the reality that my lifestyle was destroying me - and everything I had worked so hard to achieve.

It wasn't ok to spend every waking hour drowning in projects. It wasn't ok to skip workouts, shut out friends, and skip family events just so I could be "productive." It wasn't ok to allow my business to control my schedule and miss out on the most important things this life has to offer.

I found that out the hard way so that you don't have to suffer the same fate as me.

Unfortunately, I see these patterns of working too much and living too little repeated over and over again in the lives of coaching clients who come to me for help today.

Everyone wants to be Elon Musk. The real life Tony Stark, inventor, innovator, celeb-preneur, and billionaire...but are you willing to trade that level of success for three divorces, five kids you never see, working to the brink of exhaustion, and multiple SEC investigations?

Sure, Elon is changing the world. But at an incredible cost to his health, happiness, and some might say, sanity.

You gotta draw the line somewhere. And that's an incredibly important decision you must make – right now.

After coaching hundreds of high-performers and entrepreneurs, I've noticed a common pattern. The biggest challenge facing most entrepreneurs is *not* that they don't hustle hard enough or aren't willing to do whatever it takes.

It's that they've fallen victim to something I call:

The Curse of the Golden Handcuffs

The Curse of the Golden Handcuffs, stringently adhered to by *most* high performers states that:

"Work comes first, and then I will try and find time for everything else once it's done."

On the surface, this makes sense.

We've all heard quotes like, "I'd rather spend 80 hours a week building my dream than 40 hours a week building someone else's."

This gives rise to the Golden Handcuffs which puts you in a Paycheck Prison. Most often what happens is the entrepreneur finds themselves in a position where if they don't work, they don't make money, and they need to make that money to cover all of the overhead in their business.

Hence they are handcuffed to this lifestyle with a high-paying job, rather than a well run business. What's worse is that everywhere you look, celeb-preneurs (celebrity entrepreneurs) are reinforcing this paradigm and encouraging a lifestyle of "Business first, life second."

In a recent article from CNBC, Grant Cardone claimed that any "serious" entrepreneur should work, at minimum, 90 hours a week.

"Most people work 9-to-5. I work 95 hours [per week]. If you ever want to be a millionaire, you need to stop doing the 9-to-5 and start doing 95."

Gary Vaynerchuk reiterated this sentiment in the same article by claiming, *"you have made a decision that does not allow you, in Year One, any time to do anything but build your business. Every minute — call it 18 hours a day out of 24 — if you want this to be successful, needs to be allocated for your business."*

And, although I understand the place from which these industry icons are coming, I have to respectfully disagree.

Yes, if you want to be successful, build a lasting business, and create legacy wealth--the kind of wealth that will go on for generations after you die--you *must* work hard. In fact, you'll need to work harder than 95% of the population.

But we often forget that "working hard" does not always equate to "working more hours."

And, more importantly, we forget that having a successful, even wildly profitable business does not equate to having a successful and happy *life*.

I've worked with hundreds of entrepreneurs who made a *ton* of money but had to sacrifice their health, family, and social life for decades to do it. And *all* of them regret it - and if given the chance to go back in time would do things very, very differently.

The problem is that high-performers have been so heavily indoctrinated by this "Work First, Life Second" mentality, that it can feel impossible to act in a different way.

They can't imagine a world where they work fewer than 70 hours a week and the mere mention of the word "vacation" makes them cringe - or immediately begin thinking of a plan to secretly check back in at the office without their family noticing.

(By the way, if you think no one knows what you're doing when you sneak back up to the room from the pool - because you forgot something for the 17th time - you're as naive as you are addicted to work.)

When you look at the realities in your life and the lives of these so-called high performers, it's easy to see that this paradigm isn't just unsustainable, it's counterproductive. And later in this book, I'll be sharing both the research and anecdotal evidence to prove this.

The simple truth is that there is more to your life than simply adding another 'o' to the bottom line. Although you might get massive amounts of fulfillment and personal satisfaction from growing your business and impacting more lives, it's still only one piece to the puzzle of living a good life.

We all have dreams outside of what we do for work. We all have adventures we want to go on, art we want to create, people we want to connect with, and skills we want to learn. Right now, I'm certain that *you* have countless activities, relationships, and pursuits that you've put on hold in your pursuit of the almighty dollar.

And sometimes this *is* necessary. Short bouts of imbalance are required to build a life of long term fulfillment (trust me, I've had more than my fair share of 16-hour work days). But the problem arises when we indefinitely relegate the things that (we claim) matter most to us in the unending pursuit of more financial and professional success.

We prioritize new work projects and profit drivers and then attempt to "find the time" for the other things that matter to us. But you know as well as I do that you can never 'find' time for the things that are most important to you. More time isn't hiding under the bed with your ab roller.

You will never 'find' time for the things that matter, but you can *make* time.

Another challenge with The Curse of the Golden Handcuffs is that it makes us victims of Parkinson's Law which I first heard in Tim Ferriss' book, *The 4-Hour Work Week*:

"Work expands so as to fill the time available for completion."

In other words, if you have no bumpers, boundaries, or non-negotiables built into your life, you will *always* find more work to do to fill the void and vacuum. You'll mire yourself in busy work and perfectionism out of a perverse need to appear "busy" without realizing that you are wasting your time--your most precious and finite resource--on activities that don't do anything to drive your business or life forward.

Even worse, when you don't have clear boundaries between your work and life, they start to bleed into each other, preventing you from being fully present in either one.

When you're at work, you feel guilty that they haven't spent more time with your family and when you're with your family, you feel guilty because you haven't accomplished enough work.

You'll check your phone when you're supposed to be spending time with the kids.

You'll respond to emails when you're meant to be enjoying date night with your spouse.

You'll skip workouts or family gatherings "just this once" to try and get ahead on a big project, but this one-time-only offer will soon become a new bad habit.

And, if this cycle continues unchecked (as it does for most people) you will eventually burn out. Your relationships will implode, your body will start deteriorating, and your business's growth--despite your best efforts--will come to a grinding halt.

Therefore, to truly "have it all". To have a profitable and fulfilling business, exciting personal life, and deep meaningful relationships, you must flip the conventional script on its head.

You must build your business around your LIFE, not your life around your BUSINESS.

And this book is your guide to doing it.

Do This Now

Before moving onto the next chapter, I want you to take a few minutes right now to think about how *The Curse of the Golden Handcuffs* is playing out in your life.

Are you handcuffed with everything you try to do each day?

Do you feel like you're stuck in a paycheck prison?

Have you built your life around your business?

If the answer is "Yes" to any of these, what has been the cost of doing this?

> Is your relationship with your spouse or significant other suffering because you're too focused on your professional goals?

> Is your health starting to backslide? Are you gaining unwanted weight, lacking energy, missing out on sleep, or getting sick because of your non-stop hustle mentality?

> Are you disconnected from your children or family, failing to prioritize time with the people who matter most and sending them the message that "Work is more important than you?"

Are you disconnected from *yourself?* Have you ever looked in the mirror and thought, "How did I get here?" Do you feel burned out, overwhelmed, and lost because you haven't prioritized the time you need to do things that matter to you and make you feel at your best?

Whatever the cost, get it out of your head and onto paper. I know it might be painful to accept the state of your life right now. But before we can make a change and get you to where you want to be, we must begin by being brutally honest about where you are *today.*

Take a few minutes to do this right now before moving on to the next chapter.

TWO

YOUR MONEY OR YOUR LIFE (OR BOTH?)

One of my best clients, let's call him "Petey", started life as a bit of a loser (his words, not mine). He had no drive, no ambition, and indulged in all sorts of vices to distract him from the path his life was on.

Then, as is the case with most good "Hero's Journey" stories, he met a woman. They got married and Petey, feeling a new sense of responsibility and drive, threw himself into his business, desperate to provide an amazing life for his new wife.

Shortly after their wedding, his business took off. For the first time in his life, he was making real money and became addicted to his newfound success. A book deal followed and he published a New York Times best-seller, rising higher and higher in his field and gaining a reputation as one of the best in the business.

Then, something happened. Petey's success came with unintended consequences. Even though he had more money than he could ever spend, Petey found himself unable to step back from his work. He had built a reputation as a "winner" and, like most high-performers, became obsessed with being number one.

He gave even more to the business, sacrificing his health, relationships, and time with his children as he worked harder and harder to outdo his past successes. He sat behind a computer for over 12 hours a day, addicted to energy drinks and late night eating, redlining his life and his health.

His marriage, which had started out so strong and passionate, began to breakdown, and after dinner fights with his wife became the rule, not the exception, after which he would retreat to his office and get back into the grind of business so he could ignore his real problems.

Petey suffered in silence, trapped by his own success. Eventually he reached the end of his rope. On the verge of losing it all, and unsure of what to do next, he came to me for help. He knew he needed to make a change, he just didn't know how. The Golden Handcuffs were clasped on tight.

Maybe you've been there before too. You've found yourself trapped in some good routine gone wrong. Years ago when you started out the business as a single young person with natural 24-hour energy it felt fine to go from morning till midnight. Along came kids and you were able to dance around the inevitable for a couple of years.

Then one day you woke up and it felt like a refrigerator was sitting on your chest. Or maybe you started with one drink after work to wind down, which then became one bottle at night, and soon became one bottle just to get started in the morning.

We all have our vices, we all have our handcuffs, and we all have our twisted routines that can be hard to let go. It's always easy to see where others are going wrong in these instances, but when we become attached to a certain way, we, like Petey, can't seem to find a way out of the darkness. That's why we all need the outside eyes of a coach or mentor.

During our day of coaching, I introduced Petey to my Perfect Week Planning formula and it was like a lightbulb went off in his head. He realized that, with a few tweaks to his schedule and a few key hires, he could get his life back together again. He could have it *all*. A thriving business, a fit and strong body, an amazing social life, and a fulfilling marriage. And now, he had a clear and actionable strategy to make it happen.

When Petey returned home, he immediately implemented (because that's what high performing action takers like you and Petey do). He delegated the tasks that drained him most to his underutilized team. He hired and coached new team members to take on more responsibility in his company, and he built his *business* around his life instead of his *life* around his business.

Today, Petey is back to his old self. His marriage is stronger than ever. He has the time and energy to keep up with his kids. And, despite working fewer hours every day, his business has continued to grow at a record rate.

If you follow the system I'll be laying out in this book, you *can* have it all--just like Petey. But to do so, you must first throw out a few toxic beliefs about success, productivity, and work.

What Does It Mean to Have Your Perfect Week (And Perfect Life)?

In an 80 year study conducted by Harvard University[1] (one of the longest running studies in history), researchers began charting and tracking the health and well being of 268 Harvard sophomores to answer a simple question.

What makes a well-lived life?

Over the following decades, the study expanded to include over 1,300 adults including lawyers, bankers, entrepreneurs, and even future U.S. Presidents, as well as alcoholics, schizophrenics, and addicts.

They tracked everything from these individual's income, health habits, relationships, and hobbies to try and see if there was a more or less common formula that leads to a well-lived life.

And after decades of research, they arrived at a conclusion.

"The surprising finding is that our relationships and how happy we are in our relationships has a powerful influence on our health," said Robert Waldinger, director of the study, a psychiatrist at Massachusetts General Hospital and a professor of psychiatry at Harvard Medical School. *"Taking care of your body is important, but tending to your relationships is a form of self-care too. That, I think, is the revelation."*

"When we gathered together everything we knew about them about at age 50, it wasn't their middle-age cholesterol levels that predicted how they were going to grow old," said Waldinger in a popular TED Talk[2]. "It was how satisfied they were in their relationships. The people who were the most satisfied in their relationships at age 50 were the healthiest at age 80."

Think about that for a minute...

One of the longest running studies in history with more than 1,300 people from all walks of life determined, in no uncertain terms that the quality of our relationships, not our socioeconomic status, financial success, or vocation are the most important determining factor in the quality of one's life.

Yet, when you look at the realities of the society around us, most people are living their lives as if their health and relationships are the *least* important factors for a well lived life.

Almost every entrepreneur I've worked with struggled, at one point or another, to prioritize the things that matter most. That's why it's not uncommon for most of the entrepreneurs from my peer group (between the ages of 35-45) to have visited the hospital at least once in their life from work-related stress (that includes me, as told in *Unstoppable*).

Most entrepreneurs have no problem spending hours at a desk analyzing data, doing sales calls, or in important (and useless) meetings.

But when it comes time to prioritize date night with their spouse? Or go to their child's ball game? Or stay connected with a group of good friends from outside of work or 'their industry'? Or make it to the gym more than three times in January... They are "too busy" or "don't have the time for that."

What they fail to realize, however, is that slipping into this pattern of "work first, life second" actually *hinders* their productivity and professional growth instead of expediting it. Although you may be under the illusion that you're more productive because you're always hustling and grinding, the reality is quite different.

Spending all of your time in activity doesn't guarantee accomplishment.

Empire Builders and successful, wealthy CEOs don't spend every waking hour working.

And the research proves this.

Working Less, Vacations, and Exercise: The Surprising Keys to Getting More Done

First, let's consider the myth that working more hours equates to being more productive.

Every entrepreneur that I know has, at some point, fallen into the trap of the 70+ hour work week. They believe that hours worked and productive output are inextricably linked and the key to getting more done is to work more hours.

However, the research paints a remarkably different picture.

According to Stanford Researcher, Alex Pang[3], author of the book *Rest,* most people are only productive for 4-5 hours a day or a total of 20-25 hours a week.

Further research conducted by the Melbourne Institute[4], which followed the lives of 6,500 men and women, concluded that:

"...for both men and women, a 25-hour work week led to top cognitive performance. Working more than 55 hours per week had the worst impact, as stress unravels our ability to think and solve problems effectively."

Another study, conducted by Perpetual Guardian[5], a company that manages trusts, wills, and estates, tried to determine whether the traditional five day 35-40 hour work week was *actually* the best way to increase workplace productivity.

They took 240 employees and instructed them to work only four days a week while expecting the same level of output as they had been producing working five days a week.

The results?

Employees reported a 24% improvement in work-life balance and a 7% decrease in stress levels. They spent more time with their families, exercised more consistently, and subjectively reported feeling more energized at work.

And all of these benefits were enjoyed while maintaining the *exact same* amount of productive output each week.

While these studies clearly showcase that there is less of a correlation between the hours worked and productive output than we might assume, the research rabbit hole doesn't end here.

In another study conducted at Harvard[6], researchers set out to determine the correlation between vacation time and workplace productivity.

What they found was very surprising.

The researchers discovered that people who took fewer than ten vacation days per year had a 34.6% likelihood of receiving a raise or bonus in a three year period. On the flip side, employees who took more than ten vacation days had a 65.4% chance of receiving a raise or bonus... almost double that of their workaholic peers!

And for those of you who claim that you are "too busy" to exercise and prioritize your health? Consider the results of the Leeds Metropolitan University study[7], which examined the influence of daytime exercise on office workers.

They examined the fluctuations in performance on days when a given employee visited the gym and the days when they didn't. And what they found was that, when an employee exercised, they reported managing their time more effectively, being more productive, having better interactions with their colleagues, and feeling subjectively happier and more satisfied.

All of this research paints a very clear picture.

To be more productive, enjoy more success, and accelerate your growth, you *must* prioritize your rest, recovery, and downtime just as much, if not more than you do your actual working hours.

Time with family, regular vacations, and exercise are not just activities that you "should" do. They are mandatory for peak performance.

As I'm writing this, I can already hear the cries of dissent.

"That's great Craig. But you don't understand *my* life! I have too much depending on me to work 'part-time' at just 30 hours a week. And if I take a vacation, my entire business will collapse."

I understand. I've been there. I've worn the Golden Handcuffs too.

The point of this chapter is not to convince you to leave the office at 1 pm tomorrow afternoon or to immediately schedule a six week sabbatical.

My goal is simply to illustrate that entrepreneurship and peak performance requires you to put other (dare I say more important aspects of life) on the calendar first, before you jam-pack your calendar with back-to-back-to-back meetings and busy work.

What you're about to discover is that you *can* have an incredible and profitable business while still maintaining a healthy family, social, and personal life. In fact, *by* investing in non-work activities and relationships, you will actually improve your performance at work and become more productive in the long run.

The rest of this book is devoted to helping you make this a reality.

Do This Now

I want you to think back on the last six months of your life. Specifically, I want you to think about how you have structured your days and weeks and months.

How many hours, on average, do you work each week?

How often do you take time off (meaning you do not touch your laptop or do any work related activities for an entire day or more)?

Have you prioritized exercise, a healthy diet, and plenty of sleep?

Again, the goal here is simply to establish a baseline of your performance and habits. I don't expect you to magically shave 50% off your work week or to drop everything, grab your passport, and take a 4-day weekend in Cabo. My goal is simply to set the wheels in motion and help you identify the patterns and behaviors that might not be serving you the way you think they are.

Once you've answered these questions, I want you to shift your focus.

Now that you know how you've *been* showing up, I want you to identify one small way you can prioritize rest and recovery moving forward. I'll be talking about this in detail later in the book, but right now, I want you to remember that success loves speed.

The faster you can implement these small changes and take action on these lessons, the faster you will be able to achieve your Perfect Weeks.

So what can you do in the next 24 hours, 48 hours, and 7 days to give yourself the space you need to fully recover?

Can you:

> Spend three hours at a coffee shop journaling and strategizing so that you can identify the steps you need to take to accomplish your biggest goals?
>
> Can you commit to taking a 3-hour block completely off of work this week to be fully present with your family or friends (without checking your phone once)?
>
> Can you test out a shorter work day for just one day to see how productive you can be when you have hard boundaries in your life?

Whatever it is, write it down and then take the first step to making this a reality *today*.

[1] https://www.adultdevelopmentstudy.org/

[2]https://robertwaldinger.com/ted-talk/

[3]http://nautil.us/issue/46/balance/darwin-was-a-slacker-and-you-should-be-too

[4]https://papers.ssrn.com/sol3/papers.cfm?abstract_id=2737742

[5]https://www.theguardian.com/world/2018/jul/19/work-less-get-more-new-zealand-firms-four-day-week-an-unmitigated-success

[6]https://www.ustravel.org/toolkit/time-and-vacation-usage

[7]https://www.researchgate.net/publication/235275530_Exercising_at_work_and_self-reported_work_performance

THREE

HOW TO FOCUS ON WHAT MATTERS, GET MORE DONE, AND LEAVE A LASTING LEGACY

Growing up, my best friend's dad, Mr. A., would often sit us down in the kitchen of their farmhouse and teach us life lessons that you just don't learn in school.

There was one in particular that sticks out in my memory.

He pulled out a big mason jar—the kind my mom would fill with pickled vegetables each fall. Then took some rocks from his overalls and put them in the jar until they were spilling over the top of the jar.

Looking at us with a knowing grin, he asked:

"Boys, do you think the jar is full?"

My friend Brian and I nodded, shrugged, and quickly turned to go back outside to play baseball in the front yard.

"Hang on," he said pulling out some smaller pebbles and slowly pouring them into the jar.

He tapped it a few times and allowed the smaller rocks to sink to the bottom.

"Now is it full?" he asked.

"Yes, Dad!" Brian yelled, rolling his eyes and hoping the demonstration was finally over.

"Are you sure?" his father asked.

He then took a big bag of sand out of his pockets and poured it into the jar, filling every inch of the container from top to bottom.

"*Now*...it's full" he said with a smile.

"You see, boys, the rocks are the big projects—like feeding the pigs each morning, taking care of your family, and making your wife happy," he explained.

"The pebbles are things that matter but you could do without—like doing all of your homework." Seeing the expression on Brian's face, he quickly added, "Don't tell your mother I said that."

"Finally, the sand represents the filler, like watching television or playing computer games."

He waited for the lesson to register in our highly impatient brains.

"Boys, make sure you spend time on what really matters, because if you waste your time on the filler, you'll run out of room for what's important."

Over the past two decades, that lesson from Brian's father has stuck with me in a way that few things have.

But along the way, I realized something.

One of the biggest problems facing high-performers today is not that they don't know *how* to set priorities and "put the big rocks first".

It's that they haven't learned how to effectively identify the things that are *truly* important.

Their priorities, and therefore their actions, are misaligned.

They place an undue premium on the time they spend at the office while ignoring habits and activities that have a compounding positive effect--things like exercise, date nights, and vacations with the family.

To craft your perfect week, you need to gain a clear understanding of what is *really* important.

And, in this chapter, I'm going to help you identify the "big rocks" you must prioritize first, the "little pebbles" to schedule second, and the "tiny grains of sand" you can use to fill in the holes.

A Life Changing Strategy from One of History's Most Productive Men

President Dwight D. Eisenhower gave us, in my opinion, one of the most underrated tools for living a great life - which I'll share with you in a moment.

Eisenhower, if you didn't know, had to be one of the world's most productive men. He and his staff were responsible for launching programs that led to the development of the U.S. Highway System, space exploration, and the creation of the internet (that's right, thank Eisenhower, not Al Gore, for the ability to stream YouTube videos on your phone while in the bathroom).

Oh, and he was also a five-star Army general who served as the Supreme Commander of the Allied Forces in Europe during the Second World War, became the first leader of

NATO, and still managed to make time for painting, writing, and golfing (and he even had a putting green on the White House lawn).

So it shouldn't come as a surprise that his strategies for discipline and time management have garnered the attention of aspiring creatives and entrepreneurs for decades.

And though Eisenhower had a number of different strategies for managing his time, attention, and priorities, there is one strategy that stands above the rest.

This remarkably simple strategy, introduced to me by the late Stephen Covey, has been one of the foundational tools I've used throughout my two decades as an entrepreneur.

It's not the only strategy you'll need to achieve a Perfect Week, but it will provide a powerful decision making framework to help you increase your income and impact while working less. When paired with the other tools I'll be sharing in this book, it has the power to transform nearly every aspect of your life for the better.

The Eisenhower Matrix: The Bedrock of True Productivity

To get started with this strategy, you are first going to revert back to one of my favorite tools, something I call the "brain dump."

Put away your phone and pull out a pen and a sheet of paper. Next, write down *every* task, activity, obligation, hobby, and standing appointment (i.e. meetings) you either currently do or have or would like to do or have on a weekly basis.

I mean everything.

From date night to dance lessons to weekly meetings to morning runs to writing your first book to going to the gym to learning to play the guitar to getting a massage. Get everything out of your head and onto paper.

Once you've done this, pull out a separate sheet of paper and draw a cross through the center of the page, separating it into four quadrants (like you see pictured on the next page).

BILLIONAIRE EISENHOWER BOX

	URGENT	NOT URGENT
IMPORTANT	**DO** Do it now.	**DECIDE** Schedule a time to do it.
NOT IMPORTANT	**DELEGATE** Who can do it for you?	**DELETE** Eliminate it.

A Quick Note on Urgency & Importance

As you read through the remainder of this chapter and complete the rest of this exercise, it's important to understand what we mean when using phrases like "Important", "Not Important", and "Urgent."

When we label something as, "Not Important" it does not mean that the task is completely insignificant. It simply means that, if it doesn't get done, the consequences will be relatively minor.

For example, sending a "Thank You" card to a podcast guest you recently interviewed *will* create good will with the interviewee, strengthen your connection, and potentially add a powerful ally to your network. But if the card doesn't get written, or if it goes out in a few weeks and not tomorrow morning, the personal and financial consequences will likely be insignificant.

Important tasks, on the other hand, contribute to your long term mission and goals in a tangible and significant way. They may or may not be urgent. But, if accomplished, they have the potential to radically change your reality for the better. For example, writing a book might be an important task, but it's not urgent to write the book at this moment - compared to a long list of other items that are screaming for your attention now.

With regards to urgency, an "urgent" task is anything that either has a set deadline (for example, paying your taxes) or to which you feel the need to react quickly (an email from a client, a phone call, or fixing the air conditioning in your office).

It's important, however, not to misconflate urgency and importance. The fact that a task needs to be done soon does *not* make it important (as you're about to see).

With these definitions in mind, let's dive into the quadrants one by one.

1. Not Urgent, Important

The most important but most neglected quadrant on the box, "Not Urgent, Important" is where the magic happens in life. I affectionately call this "NUI work".

The activities in this quadrant are what allow you to get ahead, make more money, and leave a lasting legacy. Ignore this quadrant at your own peril.

In this box, you're going to write down every task that is *important*--it adds value to your life and furthers your mission--but not urgent.

These are the things that are an essential part of your mission and the goals you have for your lifetime, but don't necessarily have to be done right now.

For example, you might put: Write the book you've always wanted to write, go to a Toastmasters class to become a better public speaker, take stand-up comedy or Improv classes to become an *amazing* public speaker, start a side business so that you can get out of the rat race, hire a business coach to take your side hustle to the next level, or sit down with your spouse or partner to plan out your Perfect Week.

2. Urgent, Important

The next quadrant of this matrix, much like the name suggests are all of the tasks and activities from your brain dump that are both urgent (they have a looming deadline) and important (they add real value to your life and business).

For example, I had a CEO client working on getting an order for over 100 million straws from a big distributor (his company sells environmentally friendly alternatives to traditional plasticware).

The CEO had a family holiday planned for the upcoming Wednesday, so we prepared a plan for him to fly from the East Coast to the Midwest on Sunday so he could meet the executive team of the distribution company first thing on Monday morning, close the deal, and get back home in time to meet up with his family and head to Hawaii for 10 days.

That's urgent, *and* important.

So if you have a sales call with a new prospect who has the potential to add 20% to your bottom line, put that here. Similarly, things like preparing to host your weekly team meeting to keep your organization on track, submitting a proposal to investors to secure funding, and getting your company's finances in order for tax season go here as well.

In addition to things that are *professionally* important, you're also going to write down anything that is *personally* important. Things like planning your spouse's birthday party, or attending your child's soccer game, or calling your mom to ask about her trip to the doctor--although unlikely to increase your income or add an extra 'o' to your bank balance--should be treated the same way that you treat any urgent and important business-related task.

3. Urgent, Not Important

In the third box, write down everything from your brain dump that is *urgent* but not important (which will probably be a significant number of tasks and activities).

This might include buying a highly recommended book from Amazon (that will probably sit around unread for months), getting a new stand-up desk for your office, or upgrading your phone to the latest-and-greatest.

On a personal level, things like going in for your yearly teeth cleaning, grabbing lunch with a friend, or returning a faulty book shelf to IKEA would fall under this category.

4. Not Urgent, Not Important

Now, we arrive at my least favorite of the four quadrants, "Not Urgent, Not Important." Unfortunately, the vast majority of people spend most of their time engaged in these non-urgent, unimportant tasks (which is why so many people are struckling - stuck and struggling).

Things like playing Candy Crush or other games on your phone, watching that second and third and fourth episode of a Netflix original at night, watching Final Four basketball games, checking ESPN or Pinterest seven times a day, or sweeping the sidewalk in front of your house all go here.

The Four D's: How to Turn Clarity Into Action

Now that you have filled out the matrix and given every task in your life a place inside of these four quadrants, the next step is to transform this clarity into meaningful action that will propel you towards your perfect week and perfect life.

Specifically, you are going to use something called the "Four D's" to take appropriate action on each item you listed above.

1. Not Urgent, Important: Decide and Do

Listen. No one can force you to do the things that are most important to your life and future.

If you never write your book, launch that side business, or craft that keynote speech and practice until it's perfect, no one else will care. Your customers will never know that you're not pursuing your dreams and it's unlikely that your spouse will leave you because you aren't writing the novel you always talk about.

As such, you must take matters into your own hands. You know the things that matter most to you, the things that you "can't not do" during your life. This is your *"Life's Legacy Bucket List"*, and *you* must decide to make these action items a priority and do whatever it takes to accomplish them.

Once you've identified your Not Urgent, Important (or NUI) tasks, you must now put each on your calendar and intentionally make the time to pursue them.

In the next chapter, I'll be sharing a simple strategy called "Magic Time" that you can use to make massive progress on your NUI "legacy work" in as little as fifteen minutes a day, but until we get to that, I simply want you to commit to devoting the first 15-90 minutes of your days (including Saturdays) to this work.

Until you have taken action on your legacy work you *do not* touch anything else. This is your life and *you* must make the decision to prioritize the things that matter to you and *make* time for them no matter what.

2. Urgent and Important: Do (After Your NUI Work)

For items that are both urgent and important, you will either do them *immediately* (assuming you've already done your NUI work) or, for tasks that require longer than a few hours for completion, schedule out the time to complete these tasks this week.

No waiting, hesitating, or procrastinating. Simply sit down and get to work or identify a time in the near future where you will tackle these items.

3. Not Important, Urgent: Delegate

To make the most of the Eisenhower matrix and achieve the freedom and lifestyle you desire, you must delegate every task that is not important, but urgent.

Now I know what you're thinking. "But Craig, that costs money!"

Listen, I'm going to be blunt. If you want to build an empire and create a lasting legacy, you *cannot* do it alone. One of the *biggest* mistakes I see entrepreneurs making is that they rarely ask for help and when they do, it's typically too late.

Everything in life is going to cost you something. It might cost you money, time, or ... your dreams. And I can't let you penny pinch your way into frustration.

If you have the financial means, I *strongly* encourage you to hire a part or full time assistant to whom you can outsource your most troublesome and draining tasks. My assistant saves me, on average, over 25 hours of busywork each week. If it wasn't for her - and the rest of my team - then I would never have been able to write this book, hold my life-changing events, workshops, and seminars, or achieve my big goals and dreams (while helping you achieve yours).

Realize that hiring new team members--or even professional help like a chef, personal trainer, or house keeper, or nanny--is not an expense, but an investment in your future and your sanity.

If necessary, cut back on other expenses (do you really need two cars - and two car payments - when you can just use Uber?). Use these savings to invest in help so you can make time and energy for more important matters - ultimately allowing you to make more money and have a bigger impact.

Once you have your team in place, it's time to delegate. Have your assistant send out your thank you emails, book flights, and schedule content for your website or email list.

Instead of wasting an entire afternoon (that could have been spent building your Empire or recharging your batteries) on house work and maintaining your lawn, fork over a few hundred dollars and pay someone else to do it.

Remember, just because it has to be done does *not* mean it has to be done by you.

By delegating every item in the "Not Important, Urgent" box, you'll take a massive step toward reclaiming control of your life and experiencing the freedom you desire.

4. Not Important, Not Urgent: Delete

Famous management expert and business guru Peter Drucker, had many great quotes, including:

"There is nothing so useless as doing efficiently what shouldn't be done at all."

And he's right. The majority of people waste *hours* every single day trying to do tasks efficiently that should not be done at all.

These include, but are certainly not limited to:

> Seeking the approval of others for doing things that do not serve your life;

Building out inconsequential marketing funnels or social media pages that won't have a significant impact on your business's bottom line

Being obsessed with getting to inbox zero or listening to every single back episode of a new podcast you've discovered or compulsively following hundreds of 'gurus' on social media, etc.

Don't be like most people.

Right now, I want you to mentally "let go" of every task in this third quadrant. If you want, you can even go as far as to pull out a new sheet of paper and write down, "I will no longer waste my time, energy, and attention engaging in...."

Success and personal fulfillment are as much about what you *do not* do as about the things that you do. By deleting the tasks and activities from your life that don't serve your mission, you will free up the space you need to live your best life.

Two Questions to Get Even More Clarity

I'm a big believer that "Values and vision drive every decision."

If you don't consciously craft a vision for your life and decide on the things that you value most, you will, by default, adopt the values and vision of society (namely, materialism, success for the sake of success, money first, family second, etc).

As you work through this exercise, it can sometimes be challenging to determine where an individual task should go inside of this matrix.

Things may feel important to you but be completely irrelevant to your mission or they may seem unimportant, but pay *huge* dividends in your personal satisfaction and professional success (like date night, vacations, and going to the gym).

To help solve this problem, there are two questions to clarify the entire process and simplify the to-do's in your life.

They are:

1. What is my Vision?

Brian Tracy, the famous consultant, author, and speaker has a saying that, "A genius without a roadmap will get lost in any country. But an average person with a roadmap will find their way to any destination."

In our lives, it's all too easy to get so caught up in the hustle and grind of daily life that we forget *why* we're working so hard in the first place.

And when this pattern goes unchecked, it becomes dangerous.

If you don't know what you're working towards (your vision), you will not only waste your time, but may find yourself decades from now having worked yourself to the bone for a life you never really wanted.

As such, it's important to establish early on what your *end goals* are.

Your vision is the roadmap that you must have for your life.

Sure, it's great to make more money, to write a best-selling book, or to build an 8-figure business. But these are all "means" goals, they are not the end in and of themselves.

You don't want to double your income simply so that you will have more income. You want to earn more so that you can afford a very specific type of lifestyle. You don't want to build an 8-figure empire simply to have an 8-figure empire. There are specific people you want to serve and a mission you want to fulfill.

So before going through the Eisenhower Matrix, I encourage you to get clear on what you're *really* after. What is the destination you are trying to reach and why does it matter to you?

Without answering this question, you cannot make effective decisions about what is and is not important and will waste years of your life doing things that don't serve your highest purpose.

2. What Are My Top Values in Life?

By answering the last question, you have already established your vision, but now it's time to address the values piece of the equation.

Right now, I want you to pull out a sheet of paper and ask yourself, "What do I value?"

Do you value physical health? Family? Financial success? Philanthropy? Travel? Fame? Leisure? Education? What are the things that are most important to you and your life?

There are no right or wrong answers here. Only answers that are true for you.

Once you have identified your values, you will have a clearer understanding of the tasks and priorities that are really important and those that are not.

As a side note, I encourage you to take a look at what you claim to value and then compare that list to the realities of your schedule. Do you claim to value fitness even though you haven't been to the gym in months? Do you claim to value family even though you work late, focus on your phone when you're at home, and can't remember the last time you took your spouse and kids on a "family date"?

By identifying the incongruence between your values and actions, you will take a powerful step towards eradicating anxiety (like I talk about in my book *Unstoppable*) and consistently enjoying perfect weeks.

Do This Now

Before moving to the next chapter, take the next 30-60 minutes to go through the exercises shared in this chapter.

Ask and answer the two questions and define your vision and values. Complete a quick brain dump and then organize the items you wrote down inside of the matrix. And once you've finished, follow the Four D's and start taking action now.

This exercise is the foundation upon which we will build your Perfect Week and until you take action on it, you will not be able to effectively implement the remaining strategies in this book.

FOUR

THE "BILLIONAIRE TIME MATRIX" THAT WILL SHAVE 12.5 HOURS OFF OF YOUR WORK WEEK

To achieve your big goals and dreams, you must realize that the things you don't do are just as important (if not more important) than the things you do.

You can go to the gym for 2-hours a day and train like Arnold in his prime. But if you only sleep four hours a night and you live off a diet of soda and Oreos, your health and physique won't change (and you'll likely destroy your body in the process).

You can make $500,000 a year or more, but if you spend it on things you don't need or fail to invest in tax strategy and accounting, you can still arrive at the end of each month broke and struggling.

Heck, you can even start a business with the best sales team in the world and killer marketing...But if you engage in unethical activities and sabotage your reputation, you'll eventually fail and possibly end up in prison (think: Wolf of Wall Street).

You can have a bulletproof plan for success and wake up knowing exactly what needs to be accomplished to move you towards your big goals and dreams...But if you allow yourself to get distracted by information, side hustles, and requests on your time that don't serve your ultimate vision... you'll never achieve your goals or execute on the plan you've created.

To prevent this from happening, you must "Be the Oprah of your business" using something I call the *Billionaire Time Matrix.*

Do you think Oprah runs to the supermarket for a fresh bag of avocados, edits her own videos, checks her inbox, or spends hours a day mired in administrative work?

Of course not! She's Oprah. And, as the CEO of You Inc., you must become the Oprah of your own business. You are the superstar and you must treat yourself as such.

You must create a clear list of boundaries and parameters that determine what habits and activities you will or will not allow into your life. You must learn how to protect your time, energy, and attention so that you can focus on what matters instead of getting lost in a sea of busy work.

If you read my book, *The Perfect Day Formula*, you're already familiar with the concept of creating a "Not to Do List" and have probably created your own list in the past.

However, the structure I'm about to give you with my "Billionaire Time Matrix" is different than anything you've seen before. By using the insights you gained from completing the exercises laid out in the last chapter, we are going to create a comprehensive plan to eliminate--or at the very least, significantly reduce--everything in your life that is not serving your highest vision.

1. Eradicate What You Hate

The first step to reducing the hours you work, reclaiming control of your schedule, and consistently experiencing *your* perfect weeks is to stop doing the work that you hate. Shocking, I know.

Look, there will always be aspects of your business that you don't enjoy but have to do (these include calls with your accountant and lawyer, re-reading marketing promotions for the umpteenth time before they go out the door, or making another sales call after your 10th "no" in a row).

Work won't always be fun. This is an inescapable part of business and life. However, there is a fundamental difference between necessary evils that help you grow and unnecessary tasks that drain your mental and emotional reservoirs, actively damaging the quality of your performance.

For example, I hate spending time on early morning phone calls. It's a big mistake, strategically, because I do my best work before lunch, and taking calls at that time (from my overseas clients in Europe, Australia, or Asia) gives away my most valuable hours.

As such, I've created boundaries and systems that allow me to avoid spending time on such tasks. I schedule all of my calls for late morning, mid-afternoon, or early evening so that I never have to waste a minute of my "magic time" in the morning.

For you, it might be different. Maybe you hate being hauled into unnecessary meetings (as if anyone likes this?) or writing last-minute emails to your list in the morning or handling customer support inquiries late at night.

Whatever it is, STOP doing it. There are many ways that allow you to stop doing things you hate. First, you can teach someone else to do it. Second, you can reschedule it for another time (as I did with my phone calls). Finally, you can eliminate it (as you'll see in a moment, we often spend time doing things that are inconsequential). Even if you can't eliminate everything you hate, at the very least, simply reduce the frequency with which you have to do these items.

Not only will you save two to three hours a week by not engaging in whatever tasks you hate, but you will save many more hours by protecting your emotions and willpower from these energy vampires in your life. And when you plug the leaks in your proverbial time bucket, you will have more energy, motivation, and enthusiasm with which to attack the rest of your day.

2. Stop Doing The Things No One Should Do

Another common trap into which every entrepreneur I know has fallen at some point in their career is the trap of doing things well that should not be done at all. This is incredibly true for my clients that label themselves as "people pleasers."

We often struggle to say "No" to new projects. There are countless "good" opportunities flowing into our lives and we often don't want to turn them down for fear of missing out (FOMO).

From podcast interviews to speaking engagements to posting content on different social media platforms to taking jobs from low-paying clients to attending far too many events because "you never know who you might meet", there are a whole host of "good but not great" activities you probably do each week.

These actions don't grow your business in any meaningful or measurable manner, but they give you the feeling that you are doing something positive, so you think, "Why not?"

The problem is that we often underestimate the opportunity cost of such activities. We don't realize how many great opportunities we are giving up to pursue the good ones. And you have to draw the line somewhere, otherwise you'd never sleep because of all the things you could do that "just might work".

For example, after I first wrote *The Perfect Day Formula* I asked one of my mentors, Dan Kennedy, for advice on selling the book. He mentioned how he sold 100 books every time he did a teleseminar. I extrapolated from his advice and thought, "Well, if I could do 100 podcasts and sell 100 books, then I'd sell 10,000 books."

It didn't matter if the podcast had 1,000 downloads a day or 1,000 downloads a decade (sadly, there are more of the latter). If there was any chance for me to get on a podcast and get my book in front of people, I took it.

At first, it was worth it. Every interview helped me tell my story better and prepared me for the big podcasts that eventually came my way. But the law of diminishing returns eventually kicked in, and soon doing a podcast for 500 listeners became a terrible use of my time.

Not only was I not making any significant progress towards growing my business or making my book a best-seller, I was losing many hours a week both directly and indirectly as a result of these interviews. It took me months to wake up and realize I was throwing away my life. But once I did, I put parameters around accepting interview requests (5,000 downloads per show only), and I was able to reclaim several hours per week and put the time into creating dozens of videos for YouTube and Instagram (that often get 5,000 or 50,000 views per clip).

So ask yourself... What are you doing in your life or business that doesn't need to be done at all? What obligations have you taken on that are unnecessary and unproductive?

You can even ask your entire team to do this audit on their activities. Chances are that everyone is doing some activity that if they stopped doing it would not hurt the business – but would save them a ton of time.

Identify these activities and eliminate them. And invest those extra hours into work that matters – or simply take that time and invest it into yourself (i.e. finally getting to the gym) or time with others (i.e. spending time with your kids). You'll only be better for it.

3. Stop Doing Things That Aren't Your Job

We've all heard the saying, "If you want something done right, do it yourself." And though this aphorism may ring with truth, in reality, it's a prescription for burnout, overwhelm, and failure.

Imagine for a moment if Oprah followed that advice to its literal definition. She would have missed out on impacting billions because she was too busy editing her own videos. An extreme example, but you're making this kind of mistake right now.

Simply put, success doesn't happen in a vacuum. If you want to rise to the pinnacles of entrepreneurial success, you need a team who can handle tasks outside of your area of genius. You cannot do everything yourself and you certainly cannot do everything at the highest levels.

For example, in the past year, I realized that I was wasting about four hours a week on uploading videos to social media and taking sales calls with potential coaching clients (even though I have hired team members to do those exact things). Although these activities are important to my business and essential tasks that must be completed every week, I am not the person who needs to do them.

And so, I delegated them to my team and added an extra four hours back to my week that can be spent on high profit activities (such as coaching my team to better performance) or improving myself outside of work (getting more sleep, having more time with family, etc.). This was one of the best decisions I have made this year.

Now take a look at your life and business? What are the important tasks that must be accomplished every week, but not necessarily by you?

Do you need to write all of the articles that go up on your site? Do you need to spend countless hours pouring over analytics and attempting to optimize your sales funnels? Do you need to upload every video, blog post, ad campaign, and email personally?

Or perhaps you're wasting your time cleaning your own home, cutting your own lawn, or cooking your own meals. Do you really need to be the one taking care of these tasks? (The answer is "no", in case you're not sure!)

Take some time right now and identify at least three tasks on which you spend your time every week that could easily be outsourced to a team member or a freelancer on Fiverr or the ambitious young high schooler down the street looking to earn a few bucks cutting lawn.

Then outsource those tasks this week. You'll be amazed at how this simple act can add hours back into your work week and help you achieve the balance and freedom for which you've been striving.

4. Build a Fence Around Yourself

Without a doubt, one of the most common killers of entrepreneurial goals and dreams is distraction. Study after study has shown that distraction in the workplace–from phone notifications to emails from your clients to team members asking for "Just a second" of your time–not only derails your productivity, but also lowers the quality of the work that you produce.

As such, one of the first and most important things you can do to improve the quality of your work and reduce the number of hours required to complete it is to build a proverbial fence around yourself. Refuse to allow distractions in your life.

Set hard boundaries with your colleagues, employees, and clients and tell them that you will be unavailable during specific hours of the day. Put your phone on airplane mode and designate specific times during which you will check your texts, your email, and other notifications.

Sit down with your family and explain the importance of having a distraction free workday and how you will be able to spend more quality time with them if they will respect your boundaries and allow you to stay focused.

If you are still unable to achieve the blocks of distraction free deep work you need, then bite the bullet and wake up earlier in the morning so that you can tackle those important tasks before the rest of the world is awake and attempting to steal your attention.

Do whatever must be done to give yourself the gift of focused work time. When you can focus on your most important tasks without facing distractions or interferences, you'll be able to accomplish those important tasks faster and better, not only saving yourself countless hours each week, but improving the output of those hours in the process.

A Quick Note on Information Overwhelm

An important element everyone should include within their "Billionaire Time Matrix" is to create a list of the ways you will and will not consume information.

Listen, there's more information available today than ever before in human history. With the click of a button, you have access to the knowledge and wisdom of the world's greatest performers, artists, and entrepreneurs. If you're facing a challenge, you can find 10,000 different solutions to overcome it in a matter of seconds.

While this abundance of information has made the abundance of the 21st century possible, it has come with an unintended consequence. Namely, paralysis by analysis.

If you try to listen to every podcast, read every book, and check out every blog article, you will make no progress and end up more confused and frustrated than you started off.

It might surprise you to hear this, but I have never listened to a podcast in my entire life. Despite co-hosting one of the top 50 business podcasts on iTunes (the Empire Podcast Show with Bedros Keuilian), I do not allow myself to get sucked into the podcast trap.

Instead, I seek feedback from my coaches, mentors and peers that I trust instead of spending three hours a day listening to (often conflicting) advice from people I don't personally know - and who don't know my situation. I've learned to be very selective with the quality and quantity of information I consume and, to achieve your big vision, so must you.

As a part of your matrix I want you to identify specific constraints that you are committed to placing on your consumption of information.

For example, you might decide to only read one book at a time or to limit yourself to three blogs or, like I do, to stop listening to podcasts. Or, you might take the advice of my mentor Sharran Srivatssa and go on a "guru detox" listening to the advice of only *one* person for the next 90 days as you work towards your goals.

Create specific rules for yourself to curb the constant consumption of information and make the time and energy for *action*.

Do This Now

Once you have taken the time to identify the tasks you hate, tasks that no one should do, tasks that you don't need to do yourself, and the distractions that are derailing your progress and productivity, it's time to bring all of these insights together in one place to create your *Billionaire Time Matrix*. You can use the worksheet provided on the next page or print out your own by going to https://PerfectWeekFormula.com/sheets

In the next chapter, I'll be sharing a simple strategy to help you stick to your commitments and eliminate these activities for good, but for right now, I only want you to *identify* the things that you will no longer do.

As an example, my matrix looks something like this:

I will not take calls before 10 a.m.

I will not have more than one alcoholic drink per day

I will not speak at any event that isn't paying me $25,000 or more

I will not do interviews with podcasts that have fewer than 5,000 downloads per show

These parameters prevent me from getting distracted by shiny objects and other people's problems and give me the time and energy I need to focus on my most important priorities.

Right now, take a few minutes to fill out your Billionaire Time Matrix. And once you're done, move on to the next chapter where I'll teach you how to make this list (and your most important habits) stick.

BILLIONAIRE TIME MATRIX

What Do You Hate Doing?	What Should You Stop Doing?
Hours Saved:	Hours Saved:
What is NOT Your Job?	What Are Your Distractions?
Hours Saved:	Hours Saved:

If money were no object, how would you fix this?_____

_____

What will this give you more time to do?_____

_____

What are the first steps to fix this?_____

_____

FIVE

NON-NEGOTIABLES: THE SECRET TO YOUR PERFECT WEEKS

My co-author of this book, Austin, a driven and (often overly) ambitious young man recently sent me an email that went like this:

"Craig," he said, "I'm working 60-70 hours a week right now but I never feel like I've done enough, and my mind won't allow me to relax. I need your advice on the best habits I can implement to fix this."

Guess how I responded...

Did I tell him to plan his days more carefully? To work on a Pomodoro timer or do an 80/20 analysis of his projects?

Did I rant and rave like a luddite? Instructing him, "Block your internet, trade in your smartphone for a flip phone, and do all of your writing from an old typewriter?"

All good guesses (especially the last one), but all wrong.

I'll share the counterintuitive advice I gave him in just a moment, but first allow me to share a quick lesson...

Over the course of my coaching career, I've discovered that the root cause of most burnout and underperformance does *not* come from your work.

It comes from what you're *not* doing outside of your work life.

As ambitious high-achievers like Austin, it's all too easy to get suckered into the non-stop hustle and grind, the "just one more" mentality, and believing that 12-hour work days and nonexistent weekends are "just a phase" or "a sprint."

We unwittingly lie to ourselves and believe all of this "overtime" will eventually have us lying on a hammock under a palm tree while we sip frosty beverages and watch the passive income roll in.

But you and I both know this doesn't really happen. Even those that peddle such propaganda are working far more than 4-hour work weeks.

Once you taste success it becomes addictive. There is always another milestone to hit, another book to write, another launch to "crush", and endless reasons why you can't take time off and enjoy what you've accomplished.

This is why you need what I call, "Non-negotiable bumpers and boundaries."

When Austin, and other clients in his situation, come to me, my advice is always the same.

"Schedule more non-negotiable *non work* activities that excite and recharge you."

For Austin, this meant promising his wife that he would take her on a weekly date night every Tuesday at 6 pm. It meant investing in a professional guitar teacher and scheduling in-person lessons once a week. It meant hiring a coach and getting radically accountable for the things he claimed were important to him (something I'll talk about later in this book).

And the results speak for themselves.

Today, Austin starts his work at the same time every day and finishes no later than 7 pm every night. He has a regular weekly date night with his partner which, as of this writing, hasn't been missed in almost three months. He makes time to go to the gym every day of the week and takes a monthly 3-day vacation to the mountains to rest and recharge. Not only has the quality of his work improved, but he operates each day from a completely different state that allows him to be present and make time for the things that matter most.

Without these "Non-Negotiable Bumpers and Boundaries, Austin would still be stuck in a pattern of perpetual workaholism with no end in sight. And without these non negotiables in *your* life, you will suffer. Parkinson's Law will take affect and you'll find yourself mired in an endless list of tasks and to-do's without ever making time for the things that really count.

But today, I'm going to show you how to fix this.

The REAL Reason You're So Burned Out, Tired, and Unhappy with Your Progress

Think back to a time where you disappointed yourself.

Maybe you underprepared for a presentation.

Maybe you were late (again) for your daughter's dance recital.

Maybe you promised your partner you would take it easy on the booze at the party, but failed.

Maybe you skipped Monday's (and Tuesday's, and Wednesday's) workout.

Or maybe you said you'd eat just one cookie ... and half a dozen later your hand was going back into the bag.

Listen, we've all been there.

We set high standards for ourselves, and when we fall short, we feel like a hypocrite.

And there are few things in the world that feel worse. No one wants to feel like a hypocrite.
The average person considers hypocrisy to be a "sin" that's almost as bad as stealing an old lady's purse.

Yet every day, whether we consciously acknowledge it or not, most of us are acting hypocritically.

The problem isn't that we don't know what to do. The problem is that we don't take promises made to ourselves seriously.

And as a result, our ancient brains--which did *not* evolve to make us rich, happy, and successful--trick us into negotiating our way *out* of success.

You already know what you want. And chances are, you already know 80% of everything you need to know to achieve it. The problem is you negotiate with yourself when it comes time to take the actions necessary to bridge the gap.

People will say things like:

"I know I said I was going to exercise today, but I just feel so tired...I think I'll skip this today and do it tomorrow."

Or, "I know I need to wake up at 6 am to finish work at a reasonable hour and take my wife on date night, but man... these sheets are just so cozy and warm. I'll give myself 'five more minutes' (read: an hour)"

Or, "I know I should be a better partner and prioritize time with my significant other, but I just have a lot on my plate right now, so we'll skip date night this time and do it next week."

Not only are these internal negotiations draining in and of themselves–studies have shown that making and debating on decisions drains your glycogen reserves and depletes your willpower–but they are completely unproductive for building the life you desire.

To break this pattern you must realize that you are not the 'lawyer' of your life.

It is not your job to defend different positions and exonerate criminal (or, in our cases counter productive) activities.

You are not the lawyer of your life. You are the dictator.

As John D. Rockefeller put it: "I would rather be my own tyrant than have someone else tyrannize me."

To achieve the business, life, relationships, and health you desire, you must become your own tyrant. You must adopt an attitude of "I say, you do."

When your higher-self says "jump" your lower/ subconscious self says "how high?"

And the key to developing this type of self-discipline in your life is through the strategic implementation of "Non-negotiables" into your work and life.

Setting and then getting massively accountable to key action steps and habits every day, week, month, and year so that you no longer have a choice to fail.

Non-negotiables are not things you "should" do. They are things you MUST do, no matter what.
Once you've set them, there is no more mental negotiation. No 'buts' or 'ifs' or 'are you sure's?'.

You simply identify what must be done and do it.

Let's take a look at some of the strategic ways you can implement non-negotiables into your life to drive more success, balance, and freedom.

1. Use Non-Negotiables to Eliminate the Need for Discipline

One of the first, and most important ways you can use non-negotiables to improve your life is by setting non-negotiables that eliminate the need for discipline and willpower.

If you are strategic with your commitments, you will find that there are certain "cornerstone" habits and non-negotiables that make everything else in your life easier.

For example, my personal non-negotiables are:

I do not swear.

I never, ever hit "snooze".

I write for 90 minutes per day.

I meditate for 10 minutes per day.

I consume five servings of greens every day.

I drink 1.5 liters of water within the first hour of waking up.

(Just writing those down and getting public accountability from you strengthens my resolve to stick to these - so thank you in advance!)

For me, these cornerstone non-negotiables make the hardest parts of achieving my goals 10X easier and reduce my need for willpower or motivation.

If I don't hit snooze then I can sit down to write for the first 90-minutes of my day .

If I consume my five servings of greens every day and 1.5 liters of water, I feel better, think better, and move better all day long.

If I do my 10-minutes of meditation daily, I'm less likely to slip back into anxiety, avoid envious thoughts, and more likely to stay focused at work.

These non-negotiables "trickle down" and create a virtuous cycle that makes it easy to stick to my other positive habits *without* requiring Herculean mental effort.

But what about you?

What are the things you struggle with most on a weekly basis and how can you intentionally set non-negotiables to eliminate that struggle and make success automatic?

For example, if you struggle with binge eating late at night, setting two non-negotiables like: "I eat at least four meals with 30 grams of protein during the day so that I can stop eating at 7 pm" and "I do not keep junk food at my house" will make success easy. If you eat enough of the right things during the day and refuse to let your pantry turn into Willy Wonka's Chocolate Factory, you won't need to exert willpower late at night.

Or, if you struggle to stay focused during the work day because you get sucked into the vortex of new YouTube videos, articles, and Instagram posts, you can set the non-negotiable, "I block every non-work website and application from 9 am until 5 pm". If you literally cannot access your biggest distractions, then focus and productivity become automatic.

Identify one non-negotiable that you can implement into each important area of your life to make success more automatic and keep them in mind as you read the rest of this chapter.

2. Use Non-Negotiables to Build "Spiritual Callouses"

The great Tony Robbins has a "weird" non-negotiable routine that he has followed every single morning for the past few decades. As soon as he wakes up and before he does anything else, he walks outside of his home, stands next to a 9' cold plunge pool set to 56 degrees...and jumps in.

No hesitation, no negotiation, no thinking about it. He says, he does. Period.

For Tony, this non-negotiable isn't about creating boundaries or reducing his need for discipline, but building "spiritual callouses."

First thing every morning, he does something he does not want to do. And this simple action, after being repeated for months, years, and decades, has built emotional resilience and spiritual toughness that he uses to excel in other areas of his life.

By making it a non-negotiable to do something hard, something painful, something uncomfortable every single morning, he has conditioned himself to eliminate all negotiation from his mind.

And this conditioning has allowed him to become the powerhouse entrepreneur, speaker, and philanthropist we all know and admire today.

As Aristotle said, "We are what we repeatedly do. Excellence, therefore, is not an act, but a habit."

If you set up non-negotiables in your life that force you to embrace discomfort and pain on a daily basis, you will have an easier time embracing and overcoming greater discomforts as they arise throughout the day.

However, if you allow yourself to shirk discomfort, to take the easy way out, to negotiate with yourself and say, "Yeah, I know I *said* I was going to [take a cold shower, workout, wake up early], but I just don't feel like it right now." then guess what? You will carry this same pattern of being into *everything* else in your life.

By treating your mind like a muscle and commit to doing a few "mental reps" every day, you will quickly condition greater levels of mental toughness, fortitude, and resilience.

So let me ask you. What is one non-negotiable to which you are willing to commit that will help you build spiritual callouses and condition your mind?

The key to effectively leveraging these types of non-negotiables is to identify something you *genuinely* do not want to do (bonus points if there are positive benefits to the habit outside of embracing the suck factor) and then commit to doing it every day.

For example, my friend, business partner, and client Bedros Keuilian, spent the first few decades of his life believing the lie that he "wasn't a morning person." After his late mornings started to interfere with his personal and professional life, I challenged Bedros to start waking up earlier to get a head start on his day (something he details on page 54 of his book *Man Up*).

Even though he *still* doesn't enjoy waking up at 5 am, he does so every single day because this simple habit not only helps him be more effective, but it forces him to start his day by doing something hard and uncomfortable.

It doesn't matter what habit you commit to. What matters is that you commit to doing something every single day that builds your willpower muscle and helps you train your mind and body to obey your commands even especially when you don't want to.

3. Non-Negotiables Provide "Bumpers" to Keep Your Life Out of the Gutter

Another friend, business partner, and coaching client, Daniel Woodrum, spent years trapped in a vicious cycle of workaholism. He and his wife Brittney always 'wanted' to have more time together. They would *talk* about the dates they wanted to go on, the adventures they wanted to share, and the experiences they wanted to have together.

But that was all they did...talk.

They didn't schedule their commitments. They didn't get accountable to each other or to their team. And, as a result, they spent *years* neglecting their relationship while they pursued success.

As the years went on, they realized that they *had* to make a change. They knew that the habits they'd adopted would never lead to the relationship or the life they desired and they came to me for help.

When they did, I gave them a simple piece of advice.

"Put your commitments in the calendars and set up painful consequences for failure."

And they did. The first step Daniel and Brittney took was to set up a weekly date night and let everyone on their team know that they would not be available during that time. They got accountable to each other, to me, and to their teams and, as a result, started spending consistent quality time with each other on a weekly basis.

But then, they took it to the next level.

Daniel and Brittney realized that, because they are partners in two Fit Body Boot Camp franchises in South Carolina, they would often spend all of their "time off" talking about the business and how they could continue to grow it.

There was no separation between work and home life and it was starting to exhaust them both.

So, they bought a huge mason's jar, placed it on their kitchen counter, and agreed to put $5 into the jar *anytime* one of them talked about work after their day was supposed to be over (they also agreed to donate all of the money in the jar at the end of every week).

After a few weeks of filling the jar to the brim, they successfully broke their bad habit of working when they played and today, they have one of the most inspiring marriages I've ever seen. The simple non-negotiables they put into their lives allowed them to strengthen their relationship with each other and their children *while* growing their locations to over $50,000/month in revenue.

For them, these non-negotiables aren't about building spiritual calluses or eliminating the need for discipline. Instead, they serve as "bumpers" to keep their life (and relationship) out of the gutter.

Think about it like this. If you were to take a 7-year old bowling, you wouldn't just give them a ball and tell them to roll it down the lane. You'd have the attendants put up the gutter to ensure that the ball made it all the way down to the pins instead of spending the entire night rolling into the gutter.

Your life is the same way.

As an entrepreneur and high-performer, you're not like "normal" people. Normal people do *not* live to work. They plan their weeks around fun and exciting adventures (or their favorite Netflix series) and they go to work out of obligation and necessity.

For us Empire Builders, it's a different story. You need to intentionally design your life so that you have non-work non-negotiable activities you *enjoy* doing. Without them, you will default to work mode and find a way to stay "busy" even when it doesn't serve you.

My challenge to you is simple. Right now, I want you to think of 2-3 things you *love* doing. Think back to when you were a little kid. What did you do in your free time? What activities did you look forward to after your school work was done?

Did you curl up and get lost in the pages of Harry Potter or Lord of the Rings? Did you play games with friends? Did you paint, sing, or dance?

Use those activities as a guide to help you find the things with which you can fill your time when you aren't working. Make a list of all the hobbies for which you wish you had more time, all of the people with whom you want to connect on a deeper level, and all of the things you want to learn.

Once you have this list in mind, it's time to move on to the next section and create your first round of non-negotiables.

Do This Now

With the lessons from this chapter still fresh in your mind, I want you to set aside 10-15 minutes to create your own list of personal and professional non-negotiables.

Before we get started, I want to give you two important guidelines to make this strategy work for you.

1. Less is More: It can be tempting to go overboard and create a list of 30+ non-negotiables that you want to implement *today*. But don't. The key to making non-negotiables stick is to limit the number of agreements that you make with yourself and others so that your commitments are *actually* non-negotiable. It's far better to start small and layer on more non-negotiables as time goes on than it is to bite off more than you can chew and fall back into the habit of acting hypocritically.

2. Remember that it's ok to iterate: Secondly, when you're creating this list, realize that you will *not* continue every non-negotiable that you write down. You may pick a habit that you *think* should be non-negotiable (like going to the gym 5 days a week) only to realize that it doesn't serve you at the highest level or accomplish the purpose you had intended. That's ok. The key here is to stick with your non-negotiables long enough to observe the effects (no less than 30 days) and then decide whether or not you want to continue being held accountable to them.

With that in mind, I want you to take some time, right now, to identify the *most* important non-negotiables to which you can commit.

Specifically, I encourage you to identify:

> One health non-negotiable
> One relationship non-negotiable
> One business non-negotiable
> One personal non-negotiable

For example, your list of non-negotiables might look like this:

> I will do some sort of physical activity for 45 minutes at least three times a week.

> I will take my spouse on a date night every Thursday at 5 pm or (if single) I will go out on a date with a potential partner every Thursday at 5 pm.

> I will devote the first 15-minutes of my day to sales and marketing, no matter what.

> I will wake up no later than 6am every single day.

Remember, there are no right or wrong answers here. Only right or wrong for you.

Now that you have your list of non-negotiables in hand, it's time to shift the conversation and discuss how to *guarantee* that you can make them stick.

SIX

HOW TO MAKE NON-NEGOTIABLES STICK

Just after I began writing this book I adopted a new puppy. Her name is Daisy, and she's a yellow Labrador Retriever. Every day we'd visit parks in Downtown Toronto so she could burn off her puppy energy.

One afternoon as I watched her chase her friends Duke (the Corgi) and Ruby (the Goldendoodle), I overheard a conversation that perfectly illustrates the importance of non-negotiable commitments.

A young woman walking by, and talking loud enough into her mobile phone for everyone to hear, was complaining to a friend about her boyfriend.

The Secret Ingredient to Your Future Success

Top performers in every industry know something that average performers don't.

Success at the highest levels *requires* an objective set of outside eyes. It requires a team of coaches to take you to the next level.

Just imagine what Michael Jordan's basketball career would have looked like if he'd never enlisted the help of professional coaches.

Instead of focusing on his "area of genius" (scoring points), he would have wasted *years* trying to figure out the best diet, workouts, and recovery methods to make him into a superstar.

It would have been *impossible* for him to become the legendary performer we know today without the help of objective outside eyes.

Fortunately, he worked with dozens of elite coaches, including my friend Tim Grover who could quickly identify his weak spots and give him the exact steps he needed to take to separate himself from every other competitor - ever - in the game of basketball.

While Jordan recruited an entire *team* of people to help him succeed, you might not need as many coaches in your inner circle. However, you *must* have someone on your team who has achieved what you want to achieve and who can help you reach your goals faster.

With the right coach, you won't waste months (or potentially years) using strategies that don't work or chasing the wrong objective. You won't have to 'wonder' if you have the right habits in place. And you won't be allowed to slack off on your goals.

The right coach will help you work harder, faster, and smarter; cutting your learning curve in half and giving you the extra edge you need to outperform the competition.

Not only will your coach keep you accountable, but they will help keep you accountable to the *right* things and work with you to quickly identify flaws in your strategy and ensure that you're moving towards your goals as quickly as possible.

But here's the thing...

For coaching to work, you must find the *right* coach. And after working with my fair share of horrible coaches (and amazing ones), I've identified five criteria that your coach should meet before you hire them.

1. Your Coach Must Have "Been There, Done That"

Anyone can give you theory, but real world experience—acquired with skin in the game—is the best foundation for sound, actionable advice.

I see thousands of people offering life and business coaching services who have never accomplished anything themselves and you should avoid these people at all costs.

Think about it. You wouldn't ask someone who is overweight and out of shape for advice on fitness. You wouldn't ask your friend's step-dad (who's on his third marriage) for advice on how to have a happy relationship. And you wouldn't ask your broke friend who works at Burger King on where to invest the profits from your business empire.

It's the same with coaching. The best coaches, the coaches who can take you to the next level and help you compress years worth of progress into just a few months, have achieved everything you want to achieve and more.

They have a proven track record of success both in their own lives and in the lives of the clients they serve that *prove* they can not only talk the talk, but walk the walk.

For example, every year, I work with dozens of amazing clients with the goal to build a 6-figure business. More often than not, I help them hit their first $100k within 3-6 months of working together. How? Because I've built *five*

7-figure businesses in five different industries and know exactly what my clients need to do to increase the income in their business.

2. Find a Coach Who Shares Your Morals and Ethics

In a world saturated with coaches who promise to help you make money, there is no shortage of "gurus" who can help you get rich. The catch? You have to compromise your values to get there.

I don't recommend risking your reputation—and possibly jail time —just to make money.
Instead, choose a mentor with integrity. That's why I sought out coaching from respected entrepreneurs and speakers like Tom Venuto, Yanik Silver, Carrie Wilkerson, Joel Weldon, Joe Polish, Taki Moore and Bedros Keuilian. These are men and women who have uncompromising ethics, and have showed me how to achieve my dreams without sacrificing my morals.

Even if a coach has achieved what you want to achieve, that doesn't mean they are the right fit for your life. You need people who share your morals, ethics, and values and have achieved success in the same way you wish to achieve it.

3. The Coach Must Deliver No-Holds Barred Accountability

One of the primary reasons for working with a coach (at least for the purposes of this chapter) is to have someone holding you accountable to the commitments and non-negotiables you set for yourself.

Ideally, you want to work with a coach who is willing to offer strict *daily* accountability and who has a track record of being a "hard ass" who refuses to let their clients off the hook. If you tell your coach that you are going to do something and you *don't* do it, you should know that they won't let you down easy.

4. You Must Have Good Rapport with Your Coach

For a coaching relationship to be successful you must *like* your coach (shocking, I know). You must have rapport with them and enjoy your interactions together. No matter how ethical and successful a coach is or how heavily they hold you accountable, the relationship won't work if you don't get along with one another.

Before hiring a coach, spend some time going through their online content and social media profiles. If you can, get to one of their live events - or see them speak somewhere. Try to see if you share similar interests, beliefs, and attitudes about the world and about success.

The best coaching relationships are those that last for several years (not just a few months) and for this to happen, you must genuinely like, respect, and admire your coach. We've all seen great sports teams break down when the player-coach relationship goes sour, and it's no different in business.

5. You Must Check Your Coaches References

What's the first thing you do when you hear about a new restaurant in town? That's right, you go straight to Google for the online reviews. You wouldn't go there without at least seeing what a few other people said about the experience. The same is true when hiring a coach.

Sure, you can look on their website and read the success stories. But I encourage you to go the extra mile and ask to speak with a few of their past clients (because I've heard horror stories about some coaches posting things that people never said). It's crazy, but true.

By taking the time to hear from their previous clients, you'll gain a better understanding of what your coaching experience will be like and what you can expect. You'll quickly be able to spot any red flags and identify potential problems *before* investing your hard earned cash.

Once you have social accountability (friends, co-workers, family) and professional accountability (a coach), there's only one final step to making your non-negotiables stick.

The Power of Pain to Help You Achieve Your Goals

The second, and even more important, step you must take to make your non-negotiables truly non-negotiable is to set clear and painful consequences for failure.

For most people, it isn't enough to simply tell someone "My partner and I do date night every Wednesday at 7 pm."

Sure you might feel a little shame and guilt when cancelling, but rarely are they powerful enough to stop you from saying, "Honey, I have to cancel."

To guarantee you follow through on your commitments *no matter what,* you have to up the ante. That means having significant consequences in place that make it *very, very* painful to fail.

The exact nature of these consequences depend on the things you find most undesirable.

For example, you could write a check equivalent to 10% of your monthly income and give it to a friend or mentor, instructing them to send it to a cause you *dislike* if you fail to follow through on your non-negotiables. (Heck, giving that amount of money to <u>anyone</u> should be enough to keep you on track.)

It doesn't matter what the specific consequence is. Only that it's powerful enough to keep you on track and make success automatic.

Do This Now

Right now, I want you to identify at least one person with whom you can create an accountability agreement *today* to help you stick to your non-negotiables.

Before you move on to the next chapter, send them an email or text and ask them if they're willing to help you.

Next, take a few minutes to research coaches who might be a good fit for your life and your budget. Do your research and schedule at least 2-3 calls with potential coaches in the next two weeks.

After you've done this, take a few minutes to identify at least one painful consequence that you can set for each of your non-negotiables. Share this with the accountability partner you just reached out to (you *did* reach out, right?) and do whatever you need to do to make it stick (send them a check, give them your Instagram password etc).

If you do nothing else in this book, do this. The right coach and accountability system will help you achieve success faster and easier than you can possibly imagine.

P.S. Interested in getting the coaching and accountability you need to become more productive, increase your income, and live your perfect life? I invite you to send me a quick email with your goals to Craig@PerfectWeekFormula.com with the subject line "Coach!" and we'll jump on a quick call to see if it's a good fit.

SEVEN

HOW TO BUILD A LASTING LEGACY IN 15 MINUTES A DAY

When I wrote my first book *The Perfect Day Formula,* I didn't do what most writers do.

I didn't enter into "monk mode" for months on end or lock myself away in a cabin deep in the woods without access to the internet. I didn't spend eight hours a day in a nicotine and caffeine fueled writing frenzy.

In fact, on average, I spent fewer than fifteen minutes a day writing my first book. A book which has now sold more than 30,000 copies.

Every morning, after waking up and going through my "Farm boy morning routine" (which I'll explain in the next chapter), I sat down at my desk and devoted just a few minutes to the book.

Little by little, day by day, week by week, I chipped away at the project. Progress was slow but consistent and within six short months, the book was ready to be shipped off for editing.

I used this same strategy to write my Wall Street Journal best-seller, *Unstoppable* and to complete countless other projects that I "didn't have the time" to do.

Now, to most people, fifteen minutes doesn't sound like a lot. In fact, when I share this story with my $25,000/day coaching clients, they always respond the same way.

"You don't *really* think I can make real progress towards my biggest goal with only 15 minutes a day...do you?"

But here's the thing...

The amount of hours you work *doesn't* matter. What matters is the quantity and quality (and thus, the impact) of work you get from your hours (or minutes) each day.

And during those fifteen minutes every morning, I was engaged in what author Cal Newport calls "deep work."

Those are blocks of focused, concentrated work where you can accomplish 3-5X more than you can at any other point in the day.

Daily deep work is one of the defining factors that separates the good from the great.

But over the decades, I've discovered a few simple tricks to expand on his strategy. I call this updated strategy "magic time" and I credit this single habit for 90% of my successes throughout the years.

Deep Work vs. Magic Time

Deep work, according to Newport, is a process of performing "professional activities…in a state of distraction-free concentration that pushes your cognitive capabilities to their limit. These efforts create new value, improve your skill, and are hard to replicate."

And I'm all for it.

Deep work *is* the missing piece of the puzzle to take you from where you are right now to where you want to be. But even deep work misses a few crucial aspects of peak performance.

The most important of which is timing.

Here's the deal.

Deep work is great. Having a proven system for accessing flow states, eradicating distractions, and getting more done is imperative to success. But to effectively use such a system, one cannot ignore the biological realities at play in our lives.

We all operate on slightly different biological clocks. Referred to in the medical field as "Chronotypes." Some people do their best thinking and writing early in the morning, others in the middle of the afternoon, and others still, like Hunter S. Thompson, Tim Ferriss, and my uber successful client, Joel Marion, late into the night.

Which brings us to a concept I call Magic Time. Your magic time is the time of the day when you are 5-10X more energetic, focused, and disciplined than any other time of the day. Your Magic Time consists of the hours when tapping into flow states becomes effortless. When you are able to immediately get to work and accomplish more in an hour than you normally could in a day.

For most of us, this time is in the mornings.

In his book *When: The Science of Perfect Timing,* author Daniel Pink states:

"In the morning, we have the greatest discipline, intention, and willpower."

This is why I encourage most of my clients to devote the first 90 minutes of their day to their *most* important (but often least urgent) work like writing their book, building their side hustle, or improving their marketable skills.

In fact, Russell Brunson, founder of *ClickFunnels* and author of *DotCom Secrets,* used this strategy after learning about it in my Perfect Day Formula Kit. In a podcast he claimed:

"*In my two hour mornings, I get as much done as I do in a typical 8 hour work day.*"

However, we all operate on different biological clocks and even though more than 60% of readers will find their magic time in the early morning, many will find magic time occurring at a later time of day.

Finding Your "Magic Time"

If you want to reclaim ownership of your time and live your perfect life, it starts with knowing how you *really* spend your time.

One of our "stupid human tricks" is to overestimate how much work we did each day and convince ourselves that we were more productive than we actually were. While so many entrepreneurs and busy executives humble brag about "working" 12 hour days, research shows we're all generally capable of only four to five hours of productivity each day (with most office employees averaging only two hours and twenty three minutes[1]).

My analysis, after working with hundreds of clients in dozens of industries, agrees.

The solution to this problem and the way to make you more effective each day is to intentionally track *everything* you do throughout the day to objectively measure how you spend (and waste) your time.

If you're familiar with the management guru, the late Peter Drucker, you've heard his phrases, "If you can't measure it, you can't improve it," and "What gets measured gets managed."

Which brings me to the first key of time ownership and the secret to discovering *your* magic time and eliminating the distractions from your life: The Time Journal.

I unintentionally discovered this tool during my previous career as a personal trainer and fat loss specialist. From 1994 to 2015, I helped millions of people--through my Turbulence Training workouts, articles in *Men's Health*, and YouTube videos--lose weight, get back in shape, and build the body they'd always wanted.

As anyone can tell you, the *real* secret to fat loss is diet--eating fewer calories than you burn off. But another one of our stupid human tricks is that we dramatically underestimate how much we eat. Most of my clients, when guessing their daily caloric intake underestimated by over 30%.

But when we instructed our clients to start using food journals--writing down what they ate, when they ate it, and why they ate it (such as being hungry, angry, tired, lonely, etc.), they were able to get a much more accurate picture of their diet and make the necessary adjustments to achieve their goals.

Clinical research backed me up too with studies showing that food journals help men and women lose several extra pounds over the course of a 12-week program[2].

During the early stages of my obsession with time ownership and efficiency, I had an "aha" moment. If we track our time the same way we do our food, we would make important discoveries about when we are most frequently "in flow" (what I call Magic Time) and when we get caught in loops of compulsive, time wasting behavior.

Using a time journal is incredibly simple. Get a piece of lined paper or open up a blank Google Doc (or use the worksheet included at the end of this section) and create a timesheet that starts from the moment you wake up and goes all the way to your bedtime in 20-minute increments.

For example, if you wake up at 6 am and go to sleep at 10 pm, your time journal should go from 6 am, 6:20 am, 6:40 am, 7 am, and so on all the way to bedtime.

Got it? Great.

Now I want you to create three copies of this page. For the next three days (including one weekend day), you're going to setup a recurring 20-minute timer on your phone and, every time it goes off, take 30-seconds to jot down what you accomplished over the past 20-minutes *and*, subjectively, where your energy levels and mood are at that specific time.

Typically, when I have clients complete this exercise, they notice a few things.

First, they realize that the vast majority of their "working" hours are nowhere near as productive as they previously believed them to be. And I have no doubt that you will quickly identify at least a few uncomfortable patterns in the way you are *actually* spending your time.

Second, and even more importantly, they are able to quickly identify their "magic time" the 2-3 hour block(s) of time during the day when they are 5-10X more focused, energetic, motivated, and productive than any other time during the day.

And this is where the magic (pun intended) starts to happen.

When you have a clear picture of how you are using -- and wasting --your time *and* how your energy levels and focus fluctuate throughout the day, you gain an immediate advantage over your competition.

You no longer have to guess when you should do your most demanding work. You *know* exactly when you have the most focus, intention, and willpower and can schedule your days accordingly.

You'll also see where your time is *really* going and quickly identify the "leaks" in the bucket that you can plug to get more out of your days, eliminate distraction, and end overwhelm once and for all.

This might sound tedious. But if you can follow through on this for only three days, you will gain clarity into your schedule and biological rhythm so that you can dramatically improve the amount of productivity you can squeeze out of fewer working hours.

DAILY TIME JOURNAL

FIND YOUR MAGIC TIME

5:00 AM _____	2:00 PM _____
5:20 AM _____	2:20 PM _____
5:40 AM _____	2:40 PM _____
6:00 AM _____	3:00 PM _____
6:20 AM _____	3:20 PM _____
6:40 AM _____	3:40 PM _____
7:00 AM _____	4:00 PM _____
7:20 AM _____	4:20 PM _____
7:40 AM _____	4:40 PM _____
8:00 AM _____	5:00 PM _____
8:20 AM _____	5:20 PM _____
8:40 AM _____	5:40 PM _____
9:00 AM _____	6:00 PM _____
9:20 AM _____	6:20 PM _____
9:40 AM _____	6:40 PM _____
10:00 AM _____	7:00 PM _____
10:20 AM _____	7:20 PM _____
10:40 AM _____	7:40 PM _____
11:00 AM _____	8:00 PM _____
11:20 AM _____	8:20 PM _____
11:40 AM _____	8:40 PM _____
12:00 PM _____	9:00 PM _____
12:20 PM _____	9:20 PM _____
12:40 PM _____	9:40 PM _____
1:00 PM _____	10:00 PM _____
1:20 PM _____	10:20 PM _____
1:40 PM _____	10:40 PM _____
	11:00 PM _____

Tips and Tricks to Make Your Magic Time More Effective

When implemented consistently, the power of magic time is more than sufficient to transform your weeks and life in and of itself.

However, my goal in writing this book is to give you access to *all* of the strategies you need to achieve success as quickly as humanly possible.

Here are a few ways you can level up your magic time and create a lasting legacy in as little as 15-minutes a day.

1. Leverage Physical "Anchors" to Prime Your Physical State

The human brain works through the power of association.

Whenever specific and consistent triggers are present in your environment, your brain associates those triggers with certain biological and physical responses.

For example, the first thing most sleep doctors prescribe to their patients is to dedicate the bedroom to sex and sleep and *nothing* else. No TV, no reading, no scrolling through Instagram.

By doing this, your brain develops the association that "bedroom = sleep", making it easy and automatic for you to turn off and get a great night's rest.

The power of association also works to elicit higher levels of productivity.

When you intentionally create specific "anchors" and "triggers" to help you get into a flow state, productivity becomes easier.

For example, John Carlton, a legendary copywriter, and creator of the "1-Legged Golfer" letter, has a "weird" ritual he follows before he sits down to work.

Every day, he stands next to his desk wearing the same outfit–sweatpants and a tee shirt–and walks around his desk once.

This simple ritual serves as a trigger to his brain that it's time to turn on "creative mode."

Author Stephen King, sits down at 9 am every morning at the same desk, drinking tea from the same mug, with his papers arranged in the same way and then writes until 1 pm.

He does this at the same old desk in the same old attic that he wrote the books (*It, The Stand, Pet Sematary*) that I read late into the night while in high school.

King explains, "The cumulative purpose of doing these things the same way every day seems to be a way of saying to the mind, you're going to be dreaming soon."

I have my own ritual that I follow before sitting down to write any of my articles, books, or newsletters.

I wake up, immediately drink 1.5 liters of water, sit down at my computer, cue up the same classical music song on YouTube (a three hour clip of *Once Upon a Time in Paris* by Erik Satie) and write for ninety minutes.

The simple triggers of drinking water and listening to my "work song" help me tap into a creative and productive state so that I can show up to my "magic time" fully charged.

If you look at the great creatives from history, they all understood the power of ritual. From composers like Beethoven to authors like Dickens, they all created specific and easily replicable "pre work" routines to help them get into flow states and be more creative.

To max out *your* magic time, I encourage you to create similar anchors and "pre game rituals".

Whether you listen to the same song on repeat while doing your deep work, put a specific essential oil in the diffuser on your desk, go through the same breathing exercise, chant the same mantra, or even solve the same Rubik's Cube (apparently, this is something my co-author Austin does!), just identify 2-3 simple triggers you can implement into your pre-magic time routine and I promise you will have more focus and flow and get much more done.

2. Script Out Your Magic Time with This Research Backed Sentence

What if I told you that a single sentence could increase your productivity and ability to achieve your goals by upwards of 150%?

Well, thanks to research conducted by dozens of psychologists over the decades, there really *is* a sentence like this.

It comes from Michael Matthew's *The Little Black Book of Motivation,* and it sounds too good to be true. But look at the research and try it out, and might be *amazed* by how effective it is.

It goes like this...

Researchers at the University of Bath[3] randomly divided 248 adults into three different groups.

1. People who were asked to read a few pages from a random novel before working out.

2. People who were asked to read about the health benefits of exercise and told that young adults who exercise regularly have a lower risk of heart disease.

3. People who read the pamphlet and wrote out a sentence detailing what exercises they planned to do, when they would do them, and where they would go.

Here's the crazy part.

Two weeks later when the researchers reviewed the results, they found that:

> 38% of participants in the first group exercised once a week

> 35% of participants in the second group exercised once a week

> 91% of participants in the third group exercised once a week.

Writing down a single sentence can increase your odds of sticking to a specific habit or completing a specific task by almost 300%.

The best part is that other studies have shown similar results across dozens of different disciplines and you can use this exact strategy before you start your magic time to ensure success.

Here's how to do it.

Every night, when you're planning the following day, take out a journal and write down a sentence declaring what you're going to do during your magic time, when you will do it, and where you will do it.

For example:

"Tomorrow morning at 5 am, I will go to the Starbucks next to my apartment, order a double shot of espresso, put in my headphones, and sit down for 60-minutes to write my book."

You can also do this *immediately* before you sit down for your magic time and have this exercise serve as an additional trigger to help you get into flow.

Now, there's a second part to this particular habit that you can use to increase your chances of success *even* more.

It's called an "If/Then" statement and it goes like this...

Despite your best intentions and even if you follow the writing exercise shared above, there will be times where circumstances outside of your control interfere with your magic time.

Maybe you'll be interrupted by one of your children, get distracted by an email, or simply suffer from an inexplicable bout of brain fog.

It's ok.

These interruptions and distractions are a normal and inescapable part of life. The question then isn't *if* these things will happen, but rather how you will handle them *when* they happen.

The "If/Then" statement is an extension of the previous exercise where you preemptively identify the most likely obstacles to happen during your day and then write out, in detail, how you are going to respond to them.

For example, if you set the intention to go to the gym before beginning your work day but you're struggling with insomnia, your "if/then" statement might go as follows:

"If I don't get enough sleep, I will still wake up at 7 am and go to the gym as planned. I will take a 30-minute nap at 1 pm to keep my energy levels high and prevent exhaustion."

Or, if you set the intention to work on your new book but know you have the tendency to get distracted by social media, your "If/Then" statement might be:

"If I get distracted by social media then I will turn off my phone, put it in my bag, and block access to the internet on my computer until my magic time work is complete."

By accepting that distractions and obstacles are inevitable, you can proactively plan for them and prevent them from derailing your productivity and success.

Try this for just one week and I promise you will be astounded by the results.

3. Use Time Constraints to Your Advantage

Another trick to max out your magic time is to leverage the power of time constraints to get more done.

If you've ever waited to finish a big project until the last minute, you already know how this works.

When you *must* finish something inside a certain amount of time, it has a funny way of getting completed.

No matter how long you procrastinated or how much you have to do, when you have painful constraints on your time, you are "magically" able to compress weeks and month's worth of achievements into a few days.

This works on a micro scale too.

Before you sit down to complete your magic time, send a text or email to your coach or accountability partner and tell them 1) Exactly what you intend to accomplish during your magic time and 2) At what hour your magic time will end.

Promise to send over the completed work at a specific time and then sit down and get to it.

By having a micro deadline in place and accountability to someone you deeply don't want to disappoint, you'll find that productivity and focus become automatic.

Do This Now

Before moving onto the next chapter, I want you to take a few minutes to implement what you've just learned.

If you haven't done so already, create and print three copies of your personal time journal and set up the reminder in your phone to complete the exercise each day.

Next, I want you to identify and commit to a "pre work" ritual or anchor that you will use every single day to get into flow. Write it down and commit to it for the next 30-days.

Go ahead and write out your "What/When/Where" and "If/Then" statements for tomorrow's magic time and then get to work.

The proper use of magic time will accelerate your success and allow you to compress years of achievement into a few short months.

[1] https://www.vouchercloud.com/resources/office-worker-productivity

[2] https://www.ncbi.nlm.nih.gov/pubmed/18617080

[3] https://www.ncbi.nlm.nih.gov/pubmed/14596707

EIGHT

THE THREE FOUNDATIONAL HABITS OF YOUR PERFECT WEEK

When I was a young boy, one of the few things I liked about the Sunday service at First St. John Lutheran was my mother's singing. She has the voice of an angel, and I'll never forget her singing a hymn that included this verse:

"On Christ, the solid Rock, I stand;
All other ground is sinking sand."

You've probably heard a parable about the pitfalls of building a house on sand compared to one on a strong foundation. And maybe you've heard this metaphor applied to building relationships or a business.

If you're a want-to-be entrepreneur who is always chasing the latest business fads and thinking that "a fast funnel" will fix all of your money problems, you'll find nothing but disappointment. These promises are sinking sand.

On the other hand, if you are willing to put in the hard work to learn timeless, high-income skills such as sales, speaking, and leadership, you'll never have to worry about money for the rest of your life. This is the solid foundation on which a successful business is built.

Same goes for your personal habits, routines, and daily structure. You can try to implement all of the latest hacks and "weird productivity tricks" you want. But if you don't properly lay the foundation, you will never achieve your Perfect Week.

The following three principles are the bedrock upon which you must build your perfect life. They will give the unshakable foundation you need to weather the storms of life and achieve lasting success.

Foundational Pillar #1: Reflect on Your Weekly Performance with the "Movie of Your Week"

Famous podcaster and UFC presenter Joe Rogan published a viral YouTube video (that's been viewed nearly four million times), titled "Be the Hero of Your Own Movie[1]." During this 90-second motivational fireball, he instructs viewers to "Think of your life as a movie that started today... if your life was a movie, what would the hero of your life movie do right now?"

I love this analogy and think it provides a valuable framework with which to analyze and look at our lives. However, don't just think about the movie that is about to happen. You must also review the movie that has already been played. I call this watching the "Movie of Your Week." And it goes like this.

Every Sunday morning, before you begin planning for your upcoming week, take 10 minutes and replay the movie of your week. Notice what you *wanted* to achieve and then compare it to what you *actually* did.

For example, let's say you *wanted* to wake up at 6 am each morning, write 2,000 words in your new book, finish work by 6 pm every day, complete three weight training sessions, and take your spouse out on a date night.

What actually happened was that you had a great day on Monday, waking up on time, writing, hitting the gym, and finishing work at a reasonable time, but then, you stayed up late watching the final episode of *Game of Thrones* with your spouse and didn't get to bed until midnight.

Tuesday morning, you slept through your alarm, missed your Magic Time, and spent the rest of the day trying to catch up. You skipped your workout and consumed too much caffeine at 4 pm, which made it difficult for you to fall asleep that night.

After falling so far behind on work the next day, you told your spouse that you wouldn't be able to make it to date night and that you would "try another night" (which you didn't) and proceeded to work straight through until almost 9 pm on Wednesday.

Coming home late, you and your spouse fought over date night and, to take the edge off the argument, you drank a few glasses of wine. Because you were wired from working late and affected by the wine, you slept even worse on Wednesday and proceeded to sleep through your alarm *again* on Thursday. I won't even mention what happened on Friday...

But all that is over. Forgive yourself the sins of the past, and don't waste time or energy on guilt or shame. Instead, use this as an opportunity to get better. The Movie of Your Week exercise offers you the opportunity to be "the scientist of your life" and make incredible discoveries about how you can improve yourself and your structure to get more out of your days and weeks. .

Reflecting on the previous seven days allows you to establish the cause and effect between staying up late watching television or working in front of screens (that mentally stimulate you and expose you to sleep-suppressing blue lights). When you make the connection between the cause and the chaos that follows, you'll be more apt to make some changes in your life.

For example, you might realize that you need to be *in bed* no later than 10 pm every night, no exceptions, if you want to get up by 6 am. Otherwise, the domino effect of sleep deprivation will result in more stress, chaos, and poor performance in your week and life.

However, you also know that you're susceptible to late night binge watching, so you realize that you need support and accountability to enact the new changes. You could, for example, sit down with your spouse and explain that you need to make sleep a priority so you can finish work at a reasonable hour and make more time for the things that matter most. You also send a text message to your coach and ask him to change the password on your Netflix account until you've had a 14-day streak of waking up and going to bed on time.

Within a few days, the positive effects of your habit change are obvious. You wake up on time every day (feeling refreshed, energized, and excited about the day, no less), finish work before 6 pm, and make sure to take your spouse out for an amazing date.

That is the power of intentional reflection and introspection.

Although I encourage you to reflect on your performance *daily* (as I'll be discussing in chapter ten), it's sometimes challenging to identify the patterns and routines holding you back from success with such a myopic view.

When you replay the entire week, you can identify the "first cause" of your stress, anxiety, and overwhelm. You can pinpoint problems and stop them *before* they get out of control. You can make small tweaks quickly and efficiently and know *exactly* what you need to do to achieve your perfect weeks.

And once you've taken the time to reflect, learn, and grow, it's time to take that new knowledge and put it into an actionable plan for the upcoming week.

Foundational Pillar #2: Plan Your Weeks on Sunday Morning

My friend and client Sharran Srivatsaa is known as the King of Scale. He literally 10X'd a business, taking Teles Properties from $350 million in revenue to more than $3.5 billion in a matter of only five years. Last year, while visiting me in Toronto, he attended a Robin Sharma event. When we met for a drink that night in the Ritz-Carlton lobby bar, Sharran was excited to share his *biggest* takeaways from the day.

"Craig," he said, "one of the most important lessons I learned from the event is to start planning my weeks on Sunday morning, when I'm the most rested and least stressed. Robin called this, 'having a beautiful planning session', instead of rushing through it on Sunday night like most people do."

Listen, your Perfect Week doesn't begin Monday morning when your alarm goes off. It doesn't even begin on Sunday night when you're planning for the following day.

It begins about 60-minutes after you wake up on Sunday morning.

By blocking off the first 30-60 minutes of every Sunday and planning your week, either by yourself or with your spouse, you begin your week from a place of power and clarity.

Your discipline, intention, and willpower are as high as they're going to be *all week* and you are using this to your advantage by carefully crafting exactly how you want your week to unfold.

By doing this in the morning, you'll no longer stress about having to prepare for your week on Sunday evening after the kids have been put to bed and you're exhausted from a busy weekend. You won't forget to do it or decide that there are other more important priorities. When you implement a beautiful planning session, you'll wake up every Monday morning knowing exactly what to do to dominate your days--and have a perfect week.

Foundational Pillar # 3: Your Weekly Detox

Earlier we clearly established that vacations, shorter work weeks, and regular exercise are key to sustained peak performance. Just like an elite athlete can't be in "playoff mode" 24/7 365, it's impossible for you to sustain focus, discipline, and willpower indefinitely. You need periods of rest and recovery to perform at your best.

Unfortunately, and especially when you first embrace the "Life first, business second" paradigm, these larger periods of rest and recovery might not always fit inside the realities of your life. No matter how meticulously you plan or how effectively you delegate, there *will* be times where a 25 hour work week isn't just impractical, it's impossible. There will be stretches of life where an extended vacation simply isn't tenable. And there will be periods during your business's growth where 6 day work weeks are mandatory to achieve your goals.

This is especially true during the early stages of your business or career where you *must* hit certain deadlines and objectives to keep food on the table. And it's during these times where "micro" recovery becomes the priority.

To accomplish this, you are going to use something that I like to refer to as a "digital detox day".

A digital detox day is, much like the name implies, a day where you will "detox" from all electronics and external stimuli. Listen, the human brain did not evolve to handle the barrage of information and dopamine-producing stimuli (think getting 'likes' on Instagram, watching an endless stream of funny videos, and reading clickbait articles).

We aren't wired to be *so* connected to our technology and the startling research correlating extended electronic use with anxiety and depression[2] should encourage everyone to unplug and disconnect on a weekly basis.

One day each week, I challenge you to unplug from all of your devices. Turn off your phone and put it in a drawer. Shut down your computer, unplug your TV, and reconnect with life. See what it's like to go out on the town without checking your email or scrolling through Instagram every five minutes.

Warning: The first time you try this, aim for just three hours. Gradually build your 'tolerance' each week until you're going a full day without devices.

Use the time to spend with your spouse sipping coffee and actually *talking* to each other. Go on hikes with your family (take a printed map instead of depending on your phone). Play board games with your kids, pick up an instrument, or go visit friends. If a big idea comes up, write it down on paper and deal with it later. There's no need to send an email right now. Do anything you like so long as you don't touch any device that's connected to the internet (with the exception of your Tesla or refrigerator).

By intentionally stepping back from your work and your electronics, you can fully recharge and reconnect with your life and the people you love. You'll come back the next day feeling more rested, creative, and motivated and I can promise you, if you will commit to this weekly for at least a month, you'll wonder how you ever lived any other way.

Do This Now

Before moving onto the next chapter, I want you to pull out your calendar and block off 1) Thirty to sixty minutes for your "Beautiful Sunday Morning Planning" and 2) Three hours for your first (or next) digital detox day.

Implement these habits *this* week even if you don't finish the rest of this book by the next Sunday. By setting aside time to intentionally reflect on and mastermind your week, you will start next week far ahead of your competition, knowing exactly what you need to do and how you need to do it. By detoxing from your electronics for a few hours, you will recharge and give yourself some much needed "time away" so that you can come back to your work with fresh eyes and attack --and accomplish-- your biggest goals.

[1]https://www.youtube.com/watch?v=YTuElM6T5ow

[2]https://www.ncbi.nlm.nih.gov/pmc/articles/PMC6214874/

NINE

THE FARM BOY MORNING ROUTINE FOR MASSIVE SUCCESS

In early 2019, I moved into an apartment on the 27th floor of a high-rise with sweeping views of Toronto. It lent the perfect backdrop for filming my daily YouTube and Instagram videos (if you haven't seen those, make sure to follow me on Instagram[1], YouTube[2], or Facebook[3] ASAP).

I also finally found a new puppy, Daisy, to replace my ol' dog Bally who passed away back in August of 2018 (and who left a valuable message for us all in the final chapter of my book, *Unstoppable*).

Unfortunately, a 27th floor apartment in the busiest part of the city and a new puppy are not a good mix. This is obvious in hindsight, but at the time I was just so excited to get a new dog that I wasn't thinking straight. (Hey, my friends call me the World's Most *Disciplined* Man, not the most *Intelligent!*)

Fortunately my discipline helped me get through those first few puppy weeks featuring plenty of "midnight runs" down the elevator and out to the only small patch of grass within three blocks of my apartment.

Getting a puppy also forced me to make some serious changes to my habits and routines.

Specifically, the way I start my day.

To my surprise, adopting a rowdy and hyper-energetic Yellow Lab (I'm almost positive she's sneaking scoops of a super caffeinated pre-workout stack when I'm not looking) has actually helped me become even more productive and allowed me to make massive progress towards *my* goals.

And in this chapter, I'm going to share my new Daisy-approved "Perfect Morning Principles". By following the structure laid out in this chapter, you will learn how to control your mornings, compress an entire day's worth of achievement into a few short hours, and create more space for freedom, fun, and adventure later in the day.

The "Farm Boy Morning Routine" for High-Achievers

Every morning when I wake up, I immediately roll out of bed and begin my 60-minute Vinyasa yoga practice to open my 'third eye.'

After I'm done, I transition directly into a 30-minute meditation session where I chant 'be' and 'unstoppable' with each breath while visualizing my inevitable success. Then I go to my office, pick up my copy of *Nicomachean Ethics*, and proceed to spend the next 60-minutes reading.

After I've fueled my mind, I go outside with Daisy and run for 10 kilometers or until I pass out from exhaustion-- whichever comes first. Following my run, I come home take a 15-minute cold shower to bolster my lymphatic system and then journal for another 60-minutes before I--

STOP.

Just stop.

I know this isn't a popular opinion to hold, but I believe that 90% of the "morning routines" you find on the internet do only one thing--They serve as a perverse form of procrastination that stops you from achieving the results you *actually* want.

They don't move your life forward or help you achieve the results you're after. Instead, they give you the illusion of progress while stunting your growth and preventing you from doing the things that matter most.

Now, before you go typing up a petition to have me excommunicated from the world of coaching and high-performance because of my controversial views, let me make something clear.

I do *not* have a problem with:

> Journaling
> Meditation
> Yoga
> Reading
> Cold showers
> Exercise
> Visualization

Or any of the other commonly prescribed morning routine habits. In fact, I regularly do most of the things listed above and my life is better because of it.

However, I *do* have a problem with otherwise high-performers *wasting* their most precious and valuable hours of the day on activities that don't add to the bottom line or help them make tangible progress towards their biggest goals.

Remember the Daniel Pink quote I shared in an earlier chapter:

"We have the greatest discipline, intention, and willpower first thing in the morning."

Now let me ask you. As a future Empire builder, world-changer, and top-performer, how do you think *you* should use this period of heightened discipline, intention, and willpower?

To chant a mantra and journal about your dreams? Or to do the hard work required to actually *achieve* them?

I think the answer is pretty clear.

Which brings me to my new "Farm Boy Morning Routine".

You see, when I was growing up on my family farm in Ontario, Canada, mornings were always the same. My father would wake up and we would immediately go outside and feed the cows - they don't take a day off eating, you know? He did this every day--including weekends, birthdays, and holidays--no matter what, and this consistency always stuck with me.

I've carried that habit with me into my life as an entrepreneur and I credit this simple habit with much of my professional success.

So my challenge to you is simple. Whatever your current morning routine looks like (even if you don't have one), STOP. Just for a week, give my 'farm boy' method a try.

Instead of giving the best 90 minutes of your day to *activity*, I want you to commit to *accomplishment*--even if it's just for a week.

As soon as your alarm goes off in the morning, get out of bed and spend no more than 15-minutes getting to work. For me, this means drinking a liter of water and taking Daisy out for a bathroom break and quick bark at the moon.

Then, once you've done what you need to do to knock off the 'morning fog', sit down at your desk and GET TO WORK.

No wasted time. No waiting, hesitating, or procrastinating. Simply get up and get in motion.

I want you to do this *even if* you completed the time journal exercise from the previous chapter and found that your magic time is not first thing in the morning. The reason is simple. When you use the first 90 minutes of your day ruthlessly focusing on your most important task, you begin your day with a massive victory and come 10 am, you're well ahead of your competition and on track to completely dominate your day.

I recently shared this strategy with a friend and client of mine, a fitness coach and sales professional named Ron

Mourra, who was struggling to build his coaching business and make time for the work that would drive him forward. Ron is a devoted family man, and as a result, it was all too easy for him to get distracted by his children once they were awake.

He decided to give my Farm Boy Morning Miracle a try and started getting to work earlier every morning. Within a few months, the new routine paid off and he was able to grow his coaching business from nothing to more than $12,000 a month. By blocking off time early in the morning before his children were awake, Ron was able to build a six-figure business in a matter of months and completely transform his life and the future of his family.

And yes, this works for women as well. Another client of mine, Charlene Irons, was struggling to balance the demands of raising a 6-month old baby and a growing business. Each of them demanded her utmost attention and she was sick of being in reactive mode.

Now, no one would have blamed her for using her newborn child as an excuse and saying, "I can't do what Craig does because I have a kid to raise!" But after she read my first book *The Perfect Day Formula,* Charlene committed to getting to work immediately after waking up (and finishing her baby duties). And sure enough, it worked for her too.

This simple strategy has worked for hundreds of busy men and women, and it will work for you too. By diving into your work *immediately*, you will go into the rest of your day with less stress, less frustration, and a greater sense of calm surrounding everything that you do.

The 1-2 hours first thing in the morning are the hours during which you'll have the fewest distractions and the most discipline. And by implementing the Farm Boy Morning Routine, you will capitalize on this time and use it to drive your life forward in a meaningful way.

The Exact Time That Millionaires, Billionaires, and Top Performers Wake Up to Achieve Success

One of the most common questions I hear from my top clients and readers is, "Craig...what time should I wake up every day to achieve the most success and be the most productive."

Can you guess what I tell them?

Do I say "Join the 5AM Club?" Do I demand they get up closer to 4 am like Mark Wahlberg and *The Rock*?

Actually it's none of these.

While the time that you wake up *matters*, what matters more than the exact hour you rise is *what you do during the hours you're awake.*

I have clients who wake up at 5 am every day and *struggle* to make meaningful progress or push forward towards their goals. And I have clients who wake up at 10 am and run multiple 7-figure businesses that grow every single month. When it comes to your wake up time, there is no "one size fits all" formula to achieve success. However, there are three important rules you should keep in mind when planning your Perfect Weeks.

They are:

1. Wake Up at the Same Time EVERY Day

About ten years ago, my mentor and the original Founder of Early to Rise, Mark Ford, gave me a piece of advice that would change my life.

"Craig," he said, "If you want to get more done, have more energy, and live a better life, start by committing to wake up at the same time every single day."

When he told me this, I was waking up at 4 am, Monday to Friday, but partying like a rockstar Friday and Saturday night and often *coming home* after 4 am on weekends. Now, I don't think I need to tell you just how detrimental this lifestyle was to my mental, emotional, and physical health (but if you simply *must* know, you can learn more about it in my book *Unstoppable*).

The second I implemented Mark's advice, my life changed forever.

When I committed to waking up at the same time everyday *no matter what*, something interesting happened. My energy levels jumped (almost) overnight. I felt more energized, excited, and focused throughout the day.

My days became more productive. I recovered from my training faster and more efficiently. In fact, *every* aspect of my life changed for the better. I even slept better. And as it turns out, there's a pretty heavy pile of research to backup Mr. Ford's prescription.

The benefits of waking up at a fixed time include[4]:

> Easier to wake up
> Easier to fall asleep (less insomnia)
> Sharper focus and short-term memory
> Brighter mood
> Better immune system function
> Improved on the job performance

And many others.

In fact, clinical Psychiatrist and best-selling author Jordan Peterson[5] stated in his book *12 Rules for Life: An Antidote to Chaos,* that the very *first* thing he will instruct depressed patients to do--before prescribing any pharmaceuticals, changing their diets, or even exercising--is to wake up at the same time everyday.

When you do this, you allow your body to get into a much needed routine that balances your hormonal profile and allows you to capitalize on your circadian rhythm.

Although I am a big proponent of getting up early, you don't *have* to wake up at 4 or 5 am to be productive and make the most out of your days. What matters more is consistency and commitment to waking up at the *same* time every day.

Do this for a month and your life will never be the same.

2. Follow Mark Twain's Secret to Prolific Creation

Prolific author, renaissance man, and possibly the holder of the world's greatest mustache, Mark Twain had an insightful, if slightly stomach churning quote:

"Eat a live frog first thing in the morning and nothing worse will happen to you for the rest of the day."

Now, while I've never eaten a live frog in my life (although I did try frog legs once while in New Orleans), the sentiment behind this quote provides a powerful framework for getting more done and crafting your Perfect Week.

All too often, we begin our days by focusing on the easy, urgent work. We respond to emails, share posts on social media, and take the path of least resistance. But in doing so, we sabotage our days and set ourselves up for long term failure.

One of the biggest keys to sustainable productivity and focus is to attack and accomplish your hardest task of the day *first*.

Therefore, the secret to dominating your days and accomplishing more before noon than most people do all week is to spend the first hours of your work day focused on the most *difficult* task.

The reason for this is simple. When you can get your hardest and most challenging work done *first*, the rest of your day becomes infinitely easier. When you do the worst thing--the thing about which you are the least excited and most anxious--all tasks that follow become simpler and faster to accomplish.

However, if you procrastinate on this task. If you put it off until "later", not only will it not get done as efficiently, but you will sabotage your performance on every other project because you're operating with low-grade anxiety about the pending task.

Back in my late 20's, when I was a struggling personal trainer, I took this advice to heart and spent the first 30-60 minutes of my day building my online fitness empire. Within 18 months, this habit allowed me to quit my job and build a 6-figure business that opened up the doors for the success I enjoy today.

When you take Mark Twain's advice and "Eat that frog" you knock over the biggest obstacle in your day and set yourself up for faster and easier success throughout the day.

3. Defer Your "Hour of Power"

My friend Shaun Hadsall, the founder of *Get Lean After 40*, spent years of his life following something similar to Tony Robbins' "Hour of Power". After Shaun woke up, he spent the first hour of his day reading, meditating, praying, and journaling. When he was done, he would immediately drive to the gym and train for 60-90 minutes and *then* he would head to the office and get to work.

Although this routine helped Sean prime his mind and body for the day ahead, it came with unintended consequences. Namely that he was starting his work day at 10-11 am and, by that time, his team was already awake and vying for his attention. Because of all the distractions at work, Sean was struggling to write the copy for his new programs and would regularly end his days wondering, "Why didn't I get *anything* done?"

When Sean came to me, my advice to him was simple:

"Push your hour of power back until you've accomplished your hardest and most important task of the day."

For a high-performer like Sean, his hour of power is non-negotiable. He *needs* that time to perform at his best, keep himself recharged, and stay centered throughout the day.

And you're probably the same way. We all have habits and routines that help us feel and perform at our best and protect us from the chaos of the day.

But these habits and routines do *not,* as some gurus suggest, need to be completed *first* thing in the morning.

By pushing his hour of power back, Sean made the space he needed to perform at the highest levels. Today, he wakes up, immediately gets to work on his most important project (typically copywriting) and then, when that task is accomplished, he shuts off his electronics and dives into his hour of power.

Like I said earlier in this chapter, I'm not opposed to things like meditation, affirmations, journaling, and exercise. In fact, these are all essential habits shared by the most elite performers.

However, to experience the highest levels of performance and productivity, I encourage you to shuffle your mornings around and make time for those habits *after* the hard work is already done.

Not only will you feel a greater sense of pride and accomplishment later in the day, but you'll be able to feel more present and focused *during* your self-care routines because you know that the hardest part of your day is already behind you.

If you have a set of morning habits and routines that you love, keep them! But do them *later* in the day.

Do This Now

Before moving onto the next chapter, I want you to take action on what you've just learned.

First, I want you to decide upon a specific time that you will wake up every morning. I encourage you to pick a time that will be easy to stick to. Whether it's 8 am, 7 am, 6 am, or 5 am, pick a time and commit to it. Get accountable to a coach or mentor if necessary.

Then, tomorrow morning, I want you to give the Farm Boy Morning Routine a try. Take a few minutes right now to identify the *one* task that, if accomplished, would make tomorrow the best day possible. Then get to work on that task no later than 30-minutes after you wake up.

If you have a morning routine that you currently follow, commit to completing that routine *after* you've already accomplished your most important task for the day.

Try this for just one week and see how you feel. If it doesn't work for you, that's fine. You can go back to your old way of doing things without worry. But I can all but promise you that it will and the next week will be the most productive you've ever had.

[1] https://www.instagram.com/realcraigballantyne/

[2] https://www.youtube.com/channel/UClBQyeL63OdkONi5PBDY8Cg

[3] https://www.facebook.com/groups/perfect.business.formula/

[4] https://www.ncbi.nlm.nih.gov/pubmed/26580236

[5] https://www.inc.com/john-brandon/a-best-selling-author-says-2-things-make-you-mentally-fit-one-involves-bacon.html

START AT THE FINISH LINE: HOW TOP PERFORMERS END THEIR DAYS TO GUARANTEE SUCCESS

My friend and client Danny Lehr, the founder of Caffeine & Kilos (an eCommerce business that sells coffee and t-shirts...not the white powder traditionally associated with "kilos"), was struggling.

His business was doing well, but it took every ounce of his energy and attention to grow it. He also suffered from the *"Entrepreneur's Attention Paradox"* that goes like this:

Most entrepreneurs are in a perpetual state of distraction. Because they lack hard bumpers and boundaries between their work and personal life they fall into the trap of "working when they play, and playing when they work."

While they're working, they think about the missed date nights, dance recitals, and family movie nights. This prevents them from staying focused at work and, as a result, when they come, they spend family time thinking about everything they didn't accomplish during the work day.

Danny was an extreme case of the Entrepreneur's Attention Paradox in action. When Danny was working, he thought about his family and felt guilty about not being with them. But when he was with his family, he thought about work and felt guilty for not getting more done.

This polarizing pull on his attention practically paralyzed him. He was never fully focused at work and never able to be present for his kids. It was driving him nuts.

To fix this problem, Danny attended one of my workshops. We immediately started fixing his challenges one by one and applying my proven methods to get more out of his work *and* family time. And when we did, I noticed something interesting.

Like many entrepreneurs, Danny was *always* connected to work through his phone. This lack of structure around his work-life balance prevented him from being truly present at home - and at work.

Notifications, emails, and phone calls kept his phone buzzing all day and made it impossible for Danny to have the success he desired.

We used one of my more unique tactics to solve the problem.

Here's what he does. Each night when Danny gets home his daughter meets him at the door. Together, they take his phone and put it "to sleep" in a phone bed (that they made together out of an egg carton). She then plays a quick lullaby on the piano, signifying the end of his work day and the beginning of family time.

While this routine might sound a little silly to you, this simple end of day ritual has had a profound effect on Danny's home *and* work life. Thanks to the nightly "phone bed ritual" (and a couple of other habits I'll be sharing in this chapter) Danny's business has grown. His relationship with his wife and kids has improved. And he is able to be fully present in both his work and home life.

Danny's not alone in suffering from this "Attention Paradox." Over my career I've spoken with thousands of financial advisors, real estate agents, gym owners, online coaches, CEO's, pro athletes and authors and there's a common pattern that exists.

The biggest challenge facing most would-be Empire Builders is *not* that they don't hustle hard enough or have a big enough vision or the right morning routine. But that they are incapable of finding the "off" button in their brain and allowing themselves to recharge after the work is done.

Because of the hyper-connectivity of today's world, we must find a way to structure bumpers and barriers into your schedule so you can unplug from work, be present at home, and recharge overnight (like Danny's phone in the phone bed) so you can perform at your best tomorrow.

And in this chapter, I'm going to give you a simple formula to achieve this.

How to End Your Evenings So You Dominate Your Days

Here's the deal.

You can go through your Perfect Week planning, well... perfectly. You can know exactly what needs to be done and determine when and how you're going to do it each day of the week.

But as Mike Tyson (supposedly) said, "Everyone has a plan until they get punched in the face." And let's be honest, our lives tend to throw a lot of punches.

Projects will get pushed back. Team members will need urgent help on important projects. Your Internet might go down. The pipes might burst. A hurricane may hit. Black Swans, as Nicholas Taleb calls them, can come out of nowhere. This is simply the nature of life and especially the *entrepreneurial roller coaster* of life.

But this does not mean that you *shouldn't* plan for the unexpected. Quite the opposite. The inevitability of unforeseen challenges means that you must commit to intentional *daily* planning to ensure that you can stay on track and roll with the punches.

For example, if you scheduled a website promotion on Wednesday only to have your Internet service provider crash unexpectedly, you can't wallow in your misfortune. You must update, improvise, and adapt your plan to ensure success. ("Action Beats Anxiety," as I taught in my previous book, *Unstoppable*.)

As former President Eisenhower once said, "In preparing for battle I have always found that plans are useless, but planning is indispensable."

To overcome all obstacles (both the mundane and unexpected), you'll dedicate the final fifteen minutes of every work day to completing your "perfect day planning."

During this block of time, you are going to use three simple practices to help you achieve your perfect days and ensure you stay on track for your Perfect Week. They are:

1. Your Daily Review

One of the hallmark character traits of high-performers is a strong bias towards *future focus*. People like you and me are constantly projecting forward and thinking about how we can achieve more and accomplish our biggest goals.

And there's nothing wrong with this disposition. It's one of the reasons that entrepreneurs tend to be able to handle failures and setbacks better than the average person and is responsible for a significant portion of our success.

However, this tendency to focus on the future holds many high-performers back from greatness because they do not take the time to reflect on and learn from the past. And this is where the daily review comes into play.

At the end of every day, set aside a few minutes to reflect on how your day *actually* unfolded. Did you accomplish more or less than you anticipated? Were there any tasks that were more challenging than you had expected? Did you schedule more than you could reasonably accomplish?

What habits and activities improved your day (e.g. you were in a bad mood but went to the gym and got out of your funk) and which ones worsened it (e.g. you drank too much caffeine, got a late start to your day, procrastinated on your NUI work, etc).

By looking back at your performance and the realities in your life, you can more effectively and intentionally plan forward to ensure continued success.

2. Write Down Your 3X3

After doing a quick review of your day, set aside another few minutes to complete an exercise I call the "3X3" and it goes like this.

First, write down three things you're grateful for. They can be big things like closing a new client or small, like having a sweet moment with your spouse before starting your work day--it doesn't matter.

The purpose of this exercise is to keep perspective on the challenges in your life. When the bills start piling up or the payroll is late or your biggest client leaves to work with a competitor, it's all too easy to slip into a negative state and allow anxiety and scarcity to hinder your progress and growth. By reminding yourself of everything that is going *right* in your life (on a daily basis), you keep these toxic emotions at bay and open up the space you need to move forward.

Next, you're going to write down three things that you were proud of that day.

These can be personal or professional, big or small. Whether you spoke kindly to an underperforming employee, donated a large amount of money to charity, or simply powered through challenging tasks on a day where you weren't feeling your best, take a few minutes to acknowledge and appreciate yourself for everything that you do.

As a high-performer, it's easy to focus on all of the ways that you *aren't* performing at your best. It's easy to internally lambaste yourself for tiny errors and to myopically focus on tiny sins (even when the day, as a whole, was a huge win).

This exercise will help you focus on the positives and give you the space you need to acknowledge your success even when it *feels* like nothing is working.

Finally, you're going to write down three ways that you can improve your performance, happiness, and success *tomorrow*. Once you've reviewed your day and have given yourself the gift of self-encouragement, it's time to be brutally honest about your performance and look for those 2-3 critical levers you can pull to make tomorrow spectacular.

Again, these can be as big or as small as you like. You might write down something as simple as, "Consume no more than one cup of coffee" or something as big as, "Have a conversation with my spouse about the importance of boundaries so I can get into flow and be present when I'm done with work."

The purpose of this exercise is to ensure that you are constantly improving and getting just 1% better each day. Because, in the long run, these tiny improvements are what will allow you to live your perfect life.

3. Priority Planning and The Brain Dump

Now that you have a clear picture of how today went, what you're grateful for, what you're proud of, and how you're going to improve tomorrow, it's time to step back and strategically engineer your day *tomorrow*.

During this time, you're going to update your Perfect Week

Planning 7x7 Grid (which I'll share in the last chapter of this book) to ensure that it accurately reflects your accomplishments and priorities and identify the 3-4 tasks that, if accomplished, will make tomorrow a *huge* win.

Schedule your non-negotiables like the gym, date night, or a massage, review your work, and update your calendar with any new appointments and commitments.

Next, with your priority planning complete, you're going to pull out a blank sheet of paper and a pen and complete a quick "Brain Dump."

Much as the name implies, this exercise is designed to help you "Dump" out all of the thoughts bouncing around your head so you can close off those pesky mental loops that are preventing you from being truly present.

All you're going to do is sit down for a few minutes and write down *everything* that is on your mind, both personal and professional. From upcoming projects to filing quarterly estimated taxes to buying your spouse a birthday gift to hiring someone to clean the gutters.

If it needs to be done or has been on your mind, get it onto paper and then, next to each item, write down 1) Does it need to be done (if not, then mentally release the task and let it go) 2) When it will be done 3) Who will do it (is it you or will you outsource it?).

Once you've completed this final brain dump, your work day has officially ended and it's time to rest, relax, and recharge.

Before ending this chapter, I want to make one final point. Even though this end of day routine works best when completed at the end of your day, the *most* important part of this exercise is that you are setting aside time each and every day to reflect on your performance and plan for future success.

My client Eric Raum, the founder of an alternative health company, spent weeks struggling to implement this habit into his life. Eric had an already exceptionally busy life made even busier by the arrival of his first child. He found that, by the time 5 pm rolled around, he didn't have the focus to give this ritual the attention it deserved.

He was getting frustrated by his inability to make this habit stick so I gave him a simple solution: Move your planning back by a couple of hours. Eric then scheduled his daily review for 3 pm every day and within a week, the habit was perfected and is now an essential part of his evening routine to dominate the next day.

Listen, it doesn't matter *when* you plan and reflect. Only that you carve out the time to do it. If you struggle to make the time for planning and reflection at the end of the day, there's no reason why you can't complete these exercises earlier in the day or even on your lunch break.

It's the consistency of these habits that matters, not exactly when you do them (there's no "magic time" for rituals, there's only "magic time" for Magic Time!). Find a way to make this non-negotiable habit fit your schedule and I promise you will experience growth like never before.

Begin at the End: The Power of Book Ending Your Day

Although the end of day reflection, planning, and "brain dump" are the first step in creating a more tangible separation between your work and home life, I've found that many of my clients *still* struggle to turn off at the end of the day and be fully present in their personal lives.

To overcome this challenge, I encourage you to create an "end of work routine" much like the morning routine you're (hopefully) following now.

After your work is done and you've gone through your end of day reflection and planning, I want you to create a simple 15-30 minute ritual that allows you mentally disconnect from work and reconnect to the things and people you love.

For me personally, I like to end my days by turning my phone off and taking Daisy for a short walk. The fresh air, lack of electronics, and time with my pup allow me to mentally let go of my work and feel more present during the rest of my day.

But this routine can take on any form that works for you.

For example, my client Shanda Sumpter takes her son Zach for a walk on the beach. Onnit Founder and New York Times best-selling author Aubrey Marcus will regularly end his day by going to his backyard and spending half an hour walking a slack line, throwing knives and swimming in his pool. My co-author, Austin, will spend 30-minutes playing the guitar or going for a walk with his wife.

The specific routine you follow doesn't matter as much as *having* a routine to end your work day.

As we discussed in the chapter on "Magic Time", your brain works through the power of association. When you follow a specific habit or routine for long enough, your brain will begin to associate that routine with "work time" or "family time" or "kill this workout time".

By consistently following the same end of work routine, you'll have an easier time switching out of work mode and getting present with your family. This will leave you feeling more rested and recharged the following day and, of course, lead to greater productivity in the long run.

The 10-3-2-1-0 Formula for Sustained Success and Optimal Rest

One of the biggest obstacles to creating your Perfect Week is sleep. The National Sleep Foundation estimates that more than 30% of the American workforce struggles from chronic sleep deprivation[1], and I would guess that those numbers are even higher inside of the entrepreneurial community.

Despite the growing body of evidence showing (in no uncertain terms) that getting fewer than 6 hours of sleep each night causes cognitive decline, impaired performance, and disease, thousands of entrepreneurs still cling to their sleeplessness as a badge of honor. And it needs to stop...NOW!

To perform at the highest levels, you *must* prioritize sleep. This doesn't mean that you need to sleep 9+ hours a night or invest in crazy biohacking gear to improve your performance. But in my experience, most high-performers still need nearly 8 hours of sleep each night to perform at their best.

However, there's a problem. In the same way that entrepreneurs often struggle to get out of "work mode" and be fully present for themselves and their families, they struggle even more profoundly to switch off and fall asleep at the end of the night.

This point was illustrated perfectly when I purchased the Oura Ring (a wearable device that tracks your activity and sleep cycles throughout the day) for Austin to test.

Austin had always prided himself on prioritizing sleep and would regularly spend upwards of 9 hours in bed. However, after two weeks of wearing the new ring, he noticed a disturbing trend. Even though he was spending 8-9 hours *in bed* everyday, he was sleeping, on average, fewer than five hours a night.

Stress, stimulants, and anxiety were sabotaging his sleep and preventing him from performing at the highest levels. When we discovered this, I told him to implement my secret "10-3-2-1-0" formula for perfect sleep, and it goes like this:

10 hours before bed cut out all caffeine and other stimulants

3 hours before bed stop eating and consuming alcohol

2 hours before bed stop working and shut off all work related electronics

1 hour before bed turn off all electronics (including your phone and television)

0--the number of times you will hit the snooze button the following morning.

Within two weeks of implementing this formula, Austin's sleep quality skyrocketed. Not only was he spending two fewer hours in bed each day, but because of his increased sleep efficiency, he was sleeping an *extra* two hours a night (7 hours on average). And the increase in his output and performance was obvious.

To make this even more effective, I encourage you to use something I call the "reverse alarm". To ensure that you are *actually* turning off your electronics and preparing for bed, I want you to set an alarm that will go off 60-minutes before you plan to go to sleep.

When the alarm goes off, that's your reminder that it's time to disconnect and unwind. Turn off *all* of your electronics, stop eating, and start easing your way into the night. Read a book. Draw a bath. Spend time with your spouse. Do something that relaxes your mind and allows you to slowly turn off after a long day. If you will do this consistently, you'll be sleeping like a baby in no time and *dominating* your mornings each and every day.

Visualize Your Perfect Week BEFORE It Happens

The final habit that will help you increase your productivity, accomplish your goals, and consistently experience Perfect Weeks is a nightly visualization practice.

I know, I know, sounds "Woo Woo" to you.

Ever since *The Secret* went mainstream, people everywhere have dutifully sat in their office chairs, visualizing a new Ferrari in their garage. When (unsurprisingly) they come home to their beat up Kia, they disregard visualization entirely.

And it's no wonder. They are using it the wrong way. Visualization *does* work. But not the way most people imagine. Let me illustrate this by sharing a short study.

Dr. Judd Biasiotto at the University of Chicago[2] conducted an experiment to test the efficacy of different methodologies to help athletes improve their free throws.

After getting a baseline score for every participant, he divided them into three groups.

The first group practiced free throws for an hour a day.

The second group visualized themselves practicing free throws.

And the third group did nothing.

After 30 days, he retested the participants. And the results were astounding.

The first group improved their scores by 24%.

The third group, as expected, saw no improvement in their scores.

But the second group--the people who had done *nothing* but visualize their practice every day--improved by 23% without ever touching a basketball. Almost the same level of improvement as their peers who had physically practiced for an hour a day!

Pretty cool, right?

But here's the part of the study that most people miss.

Dr. Biasiotto didn't have participants visualize becoming an NBA star or signing a multi-million dollar contract to play for the Chicago Bulls.

He had them mentally rehearse, the *processes,* not the outcome. And that's an important distinction.

To benefit from visualization--a habit that has been recommended by everyone from my friend and client Sharran Srivatsaa to David Goggins, Arnold Schwarzenegger, and Will Smith--you aren't going to imagine the *outcome* you want to achieve.

But rather the daily processes and habits you must follow to achieve that desired outcome.

Every night, after you turn off all of your electronics but before you go to sleep, set aside just 10-15 minutes to vividly visualize yourself having the most productive day and week of your life.

Imagine yourself springing out of bed before your alarm each morning...

Dominating your workouts and self-care rituals...

Finishing work early in the day so you have time to connect with your spouse...

Doing the things that must be done to live the life you want to have...

I can tell you from personal experience, it works.

My friend Sharran who I mentioned earlier in this book claims that the practice of visualizing his days is one of the *most* important habits of his life and has noted on several occasions that when he stops this practice, his days feel more random and chaotic.

When you have a clear mental picture of the person you need to be to achieve the goals you've set, bringing that vision into reality becomes that much easier.

Try it this week and see what happens. I promise, the results will surprise you.

Do This Now

Either at the end of today (if you are reading this before the end of your work day) or the end of your next work day, I want you to begin implementing the end of day planning and reflection exercises. Put the exercise in your calendar and give yourself just 15 minutes at the end of your day (or on your lunch break) to reflect on your day and plan for the rest of the week.

Next, I want you to identify and solidify a simple end of day "bookend" routine that will help you get out of work mode and be present for your friends and family. Write it out and share it with your accountability partner or coach.

Then, set alarms on your phone to remind you to follow the 10-3-2-1-0 formula and pay attention to how the quality of your sleep improves.

Finally, tonight, before you go to bed, I want you to try visualizing your following day.

If you consistently follow these simple habits and routines, I promise that you will be more productive, less stressed, and more successful than ever before.

Remember, success is simple once you accept how hard it is.

[1]https://www.cdc.gov/media/releases/2016/p0215-enough-sleep.html

[2]https://digital.library.txstate.edu/bitstream/handle/10877/5548/EKEOCHA-THESIS-2015.pdf?sequence=1

ELEVEN

ACCOMPLISH MORE, COMMIT TO LESS, AND BEAT OVERWHELM FOR GOOD

In his prime, Michael Phelps, the 23 time Olympic Gold Medal winner, swam a staggering 70,000 to 100,000 yards in training each week. He also devoted time to strength training, recovery, core training, etc.

Despite his Herculean regimen, Phelps claims that the secret to his performance lies in the way he spends his time outside of the pool and gym. Namely: Sleeping.

"I really can't say it enough," Phelps said. "I don't think people really pay enough attention to how important sleep is."

In addition to getting a normal 8 hours a night, Phelps would take a 2-3 hour nap after training to aid in recovery. He tracked not only the quantity of sleep he achieved every night, but also the quality of sleep he was able to achieve.

Every remarkable athlete with a long career knows the importance of recovery. For example, look at Lebron James. If you pay attention to the way the game of basketball *actually* works, you'll notice that Lebron and other players spend more time *off* the court than they do on it.

During a typical 48 minute game, Lebron will spend just as much time resting during commercial breaks, time outs, half time, as he will in actual game time on the court. And that's not even considering the periods during the game where his coaches will *instruct* Lebron to stay on the sidelines while his team holds down the lead he helped them achieve.

But the power of rest and recovery isn't relegated to the purely physical disciplines.

K. Anders Ericcson, the author of *Peak*, studied the world's top violinists. His findings were, to say the least, surprising. Ericsson found that the difference between the 'good' and the 'great' did not lie in the amount of time they spent practicing.

In fact, his study[2] showed the best musicians spent only 4 ½ hours a day practicing their craft compared to the 8+ hours that lesser musicians invested each day.

The real difference, he noted, was in the amount of time the professionals spent recovering. He discovered that the top 1% of classically trained violinists would spend, on average, eight hours a night sleeping and another 30-90 minutes napping later in the day. And other research has found that this pattern is ubiquitous among all of the world's top performers from athletes to chess players to artists to scientists.

Oftentimes, demotivation and burnout are not a symptom of over work, but under recovery.
Just about anyone can sustain 50 to 60 hour work weeks for a few years if they do it right.

But when you combine long hours with inefficiency and ineffectiveness, you get into trouble fast.
In the same way that a pro athlete cannot be in playoff mode all year round, your psyche cannot handle an endless barrage of 12-16 hour work days and constant stress without a break – or a breakthrough.

We might like to think that we're invincible hard chargers capable of inhuman levels of productivity and "grinding". But the truth is, we only have a set number of hours in a day where we can operate at peak capacity. And to maintain your motivation and focus, you must prioritize your recovery time so that you can maximize those hours and use them to their fullest potential.

To achieve your perfect weeks, increase your productivity, and live your best life, you must schedule your days and weeks with this "stress then rest" model in mind. And in this chapter, I'm going to teach you exactly how to do it.

Profound Potatoes

"It is not daily increase, but daily decrease. Hack away at the non-essential." ~Bruce Lee

My client Isabel De Los Rios runs a multi-million dollar nutrition coaching company, homeschools her children, and still manages to finish work by 3 pm everyday so that she can spend time with her husband and kids at their dream home.

But her life wasn't always like this. When she came to me for help, she was doing well by most standards. Business was good, but Isabel was overwhelmed by her workload and never felt like she had time for her husband and kids, or that she was present when they were together.

Like most entrepreneurs, especially those that come from modest means like Isabel and myself, she tended to have a hard time letting go of 'busy work' in her business. For example, Isabel would often spend 30 minutes uploading videos from her computer to the cloud even though she had a perfectly capable assistant who was hired to do exactly that.

Now, as seemingly unimportant as this incident was ,
it pointed to a much bigger problem nearly every high
performer struggles with: Taking on *way* too many tasks
and obligations.

These little actions eat away at your time, your mind, your
productivity, your performance, and your personal life.

As I like to remind busy mom and dad entrepreneurs,
"Every minute you spend on minutiae steals moments from
your children."

Think about that the next time you are editing or uploading
your own videos, doing paperwork (poorly!), running to the
UPS store, or cleaning your office.

These things are NOT your job. You were not put here to do
the $12 an hour tasks.

(And if you're not a parent, think about all of the more
important matters that you miss because you're doing
things that do not serve you.)

The common mistake I see over and over again, in both my
billionaire and millionaire clients, is that high performers
will take on far more than they can reasonably handle, burn
out, and then spend months stuck in a downward mental
spiral as they suffer in silence and wonder, "Why am I so
unproductive? Why can't I focus?"

For some it's even worse, with burnout manifesting in anxiety or depression that requires medical attention.

What they (and I should say, "we," because this was once the case for me as well) fail to realize is that our ability to produce results is *not* the problem. The issue is with our expectations around our workload.

We make the classic mistake that I call "Putting ten pounds of potatoes in a five pound bag."

No matter how strong the sack is, it can only handle so much stress before it breaks. And when you overload yourself and your calendar with more than you can take on, burn out becomes inevitable. No matter how productive you are, or how ruthlessly you eliminate distractions, you are only one person.

So before you can plan your weeks and fill up your calendar with commitments to too many projects, you must first step back and make sure that the commitments you are making inside of your business or career are actually achievable.

To do this, you are going to enlist the help of your "Board of Directors".

Right now, I want you to pull out a sheet of paper and write down *everything* you're responsible for on a weekly basis, personal *and* professional. From going to the gym to writing emails to leading meetings to preparing presentations to taking the kids to Grandma's for dinner.

Get it out of your head and onto paper. Once you've written everything down, I want you to fold up that sheet of paper and put it in your wallet or purse. Carry it around with you for the next week and write down any new tasks that slipped your mind (because this will happen).

Then, after you're confident that your list contains *everything* you're committed to on a weekly basis, you're going to send it to your coach and at least three of your mentors or colleagues and ask for their opinion. When you remove your ego from the picture and have people that you admire and respect giving you an objective set of eyes on your commitments, you can get a better understanding of what is *really* reasonable.

Often times, all you need to cull your commitments and eliminate unnecessary tasks from your schedule is to have someone you respect tell you, "You're doing too much."

I know this exercise might sound tedious, but I promise you, it's worth it. When you get objective eyes on your schedule and priorities, you can quickly identify where you're taking on too much, when you're doing too little, and how you need to shift your priorities to achieve your goals faster.

Once you get feedback from your "Board of Advisors" commit to taking action on what they tell you. Eliminate the unnecessary, make the new hire, drop the goals and objectives that aren't serving your mission at the highest level. Your Perfect Weeks and indeed the quality of your *life* depends on it.

The Pomodoro Timer

To improve your performance, get more done, and make more time for what matters, you must incorporate the "stress then rest" model locally as well as globally. The first tactic we are going to use to do this is something known as a Pomodoro Timer and it goes like this.

Studies have shown that, in the same way that every human operates on a circadian rhythm which dictates the release of specific hormones at different times in the day and from different triggering events (e.g. early morning sunlight increases cortisol, the stress and wakefulness hormone), our brains operate on something referred to as an "ultradian rhythm[3]".

Whereas your circadian rhythm refers to biological processes that occur once over a 24 hour timeline, your ultradian rhythm refers to similar cyclical biological processes throughout those same 24 hours. And research has discovered that part of this rhythm correlated with focus and productivity works in 90-minute cycles early in the day and 50-minute cycles as the day wears on.

This means that, biologically speaking, you can only sustain *peak* focus and productivity for about an hour and a half at a time (this is why you feel like you have to "power through" after working for extended periods of time). The key to achieving sustained productivity throughout the day is to work with your body's natural rhythm instead of fighting it. Which brings us to the Pomodoro technique.

Instead of sitting down and working single mindedly for 8 hours straight (which is all but impossible for 99.99% of the population), you're going to work in 50-90-minute increments punctuated by regular breaks.

Personally, I like to start my day with a 90-minute work cycle. When my 90-minutes are up, I immediately stop working and do something to help me rest and recharge, typically meditating or walking my dog.

As the day goes on and my mental energy dwindles, I will sometimes shorten these cycles to a mere 50-minutes with a 10-minute break.

The reason the Pomodoro timer is so effective is that it creates constraints that effectively "force" productivity.

By breaking down big scary tasks into their component parts, it forces you to sit down and tackle your tasks one small piece at a time. You're no longer looking down the barrel of an ominous eight hour work day, you only need to stay focused for 50 to 90-minutes on *one* thing.

Why You MUST Schedule "Buffer Time"

I'm going to let you in on one of the "dirty little secrets" of top performers.

Not only do high performers *expect* distractions to arise throughout the day, they proactively *plan* for them.

Listen. I don't care how motivated or productive you think you are. I don't care how disciplined you might be or how hard you work. I don't care how ruthlessly you attempt to remove distractions. Shtuff happens.

Tasks take longer to complete than you anticipate. Clients throw large projects on your lap without warning. Employees drop the ball on important projects. Your spouse and children get sick.

No matter how hard you try to prevent these things from happening, life has a funny way of getting *in the way*. High performers know this, and they don't try to fight it. Instead, they prepare for these eventualities by under loading their schedule and creating space in their calendar for "buffer time".

Buffer time is exactly what it sounds like. It's time during the week where you don't put *anything* on your calendar. This time is designed to help you shore up the gaps between how you wanted your week to play out, and how it actually went.

For example, Ramit Sethi, the founder of I Will Teach You to Be Rich, stated in one of his articles that he has a company wide policy of "No Meeting Wednesdays". Wednesdays, he decided are there for him and his team to catch up on important projects and polish off anything that did not get completed the previous days.

In your own life, I encourage you to implement buffer time into every day, week, and month.

Specifically, you should schedule at least one hour of buffer time every day, either a half day or full day of buffer time each week, and at least three days of buffer time each month.

By doing this, you will be forced to be more intentional with your planning and to only take on projects you know you have the capacity to handle. It will result in greater output, higher quality of work, and a lot less stress. And if your week actually *does* play out the way you anticipated, awesome! You can use this time to work ahead on your other priorities or to treat yourself to some well-earned rest and relaxation.

The Law of Three

As we've already established, most people, yes even you and I, are a lot less productive than they think they are. And they grossly overestimate what they are capable of accomplishing within a given time frame.

A task that they estimate will take them one hour takes three and a project for which they allotted three days may take 6-9.

The problem is that most people don't give themselves permission to be human. They expect themselves to be machines and think, "Ok during my magic time I can write 1,500 words an hour. I have a 15,000 word writing project so I should only need ten hours to complete it."

We don't take into account the variability of our performance day to day, hour by hour, and minute by minute. A task that takes you 90-minutes to complete one morning may require an entire day of concentrated effort depending on your emotional state, what you ate for breakfast, and how you slept the night before.

Again, the key here is to work with reality instead of fighting it.

Considering the massive variability in our personal performance and productivity, we need to change the way that we agree to and approach different tasks.

And this is where the Law of Three comes into play.

Dozens of studies[4] suggest that employees are only productive for about 30-40% of their workday. And considering this, the "Law of Three" states that:

"Any task will take at least three times longer to complete than you assume."

So, if you have a task that you assume will take you only one hour. Schedule three hours to complete it. If you have a task that will take a week, schedule three. The point of this exercise is to put constraints on yourself and avoid taking on more than you can handle.

After a few weeks or months of tracking your output, reviewing your days, and getting objective feedback on your performance, you will be able to more accurately assess the time required to complete certain tasks and you can slowly start to phase this particular practice out.

But, at least for the next 30 days, implement this practice while you go through your Perfect Week Planning. If you accomplish tasks quicker than anticipated, great! Again, the purpose of this practice is to bring a higher level of intentionality and objectivity into your planning so that you avoid burnout and overwhelm and can sustain peak performance not just for months and years, but decades.

Do This Now

If you haven't done so already, I want you to go through the "Profound Potatoes" exercise laid out earlier in this chapter. Capture everything you do on a weekly basis and put it on paper. Keep the list with you throughout the week and add to it as new tasks and obligations surface.

Send it to your coach and accountability partners to get objective feedback on your commitments and take action from there.

Tomorrow, I want you to try working on a Pomodoro Timer. To make the practice even more powerful, I encourage you to write down your goals and priorities for each work block before the clock starts. I promise you will be amazed by the results.

Finally, set a day during the week (or at least a 3-hour block of time) that destroys all distractions of meetings and calls and allows you to dive deep into your work so that you not only catch up but also get ahead of the game.

[1]https://www.cnbc.com/2017/02/14/olympic-hero-michael-phelps-says-this-is-the-secret-to-his-success.html

[2]https://hbr.org/2007/07/the-making-of-an-expert

[3]https://www.sciencedirect.com/topics/medicine-and-dentistry/ultradian-rhythm

[4]https://blog.rescuetime.com/225-million-hours-productivity/

TWELVE

BRINGING IT ALL TOGETHER: THE 7X7 GRID THAT WILL CHANGE YOUR LIFE

Congratulations. Your life is about to change for the better.

It's time to take everything you've learned and put it together into a powerful strategy so you can live your Perfect Life.

To do that, I'm giving you the same planning formula that I normally share with my $25,000/day coaching clients, mastermind members, corporate clients, and seminar attendees.

This is the same strategy that helped my client Frank Den Blanken make the leap from $10,000 a month and 75+ hour work weeks to more than $100,000 a month while working 20 fewer hours, making time for weekly date nights (yes, that's plural), and taking his first vacation in years. (He and his wife now take one vacation every quarter - and it seems like every time he reaches out to me he's visiting a new country!)

This same simple strategy has worked for hundreds of my clients as well as the corporate executive teams of 9-figure companies, and, if you keep an open mind, ignore the temptation to come up with excuses, put these principles into practice, and follow the tactics from this book, I guarantee the formula will work for you too.

To get started, grab a blank piece of paper and a pen or pull up your Google calendar (or go to https:// PerfectWeekFormula.com/sheets). Now draw out a 7×7 grid on the paper, and label the seven columns with the days of the week. The seven squares in each column represent 2 hour time blocks that will help you plan each Perfect Day and provide you with a Perfect Week.

Now, I already know what you want to do next. Your work-obsessed brain wants to start filling in those blocks with appointments, sales calls, and meetings.

But don't. In fact, work is the LAST thing you're going to schedule (remember, this is about building your business *around* your life, not the other way around).

I can sense that this idea is probably giving you a mild anxiety attack, but please just trust me on this one. Take a deep breath and hear me out. This formula has been tested – and proven – on hundreds of my top coaching clients, from busy parents to pro athletes to multi-millionaires to struggling beginner entrepreneurs – and even CEO's of billion dollar companies. It worked for them, and it will work for you too.

Let's get to it. Here's exactly how to schedule your perfect week, step-by-step.

1. Schedule Your Relationship and Self-Care Non-Negotiables

The first thing you are going to put on the 7×7 grid are your relationship and recovery non-negotiables from chapter five. Don't worry about your work non-negotiables, we'll get to those later.

To get started, I recommend that the very first thing you schedule (and immediately get accountable for) is date night. And this is *especially* true if you're currently single and have been putting off "Looking for love" since you graduated college or ended that last messy relationship.

Like we discovered earlier in this book, the *most* important factor for a well lived life is the quality of your social and romantic relationships and you must prioritize them as such. So, if you're single, block out time each week to meet potential partners and go on dates with new people, or simply to return socializing to your life.

Once date (or social) night is on the calendar, you're going to schedule your most important block of family time. For example, some of my clients block off all afternoon on Saturday for trips to amusement parks or hikes. Others, like one of my tech entrepreneur clients, has a "phone-free" family movie night with his pre-teen children. He knows that it won't be long before Friday nights at home with the family will be the last thing on his kid's to-do list, so he's making the most of this time before it's gone.

Next, put your social events, and time with friends on the calendar. I encourage everyone to spend at least one evening a week connecting with like-minded individuals who support your goals and dreams. If you can't find one of these events, make your own. Bringing people together is one of life's greatest pleasures.

Although you might feel guilty for spending time away from work, my experience shows that spending time with other high-performers is one of the *fastest* ways to achieve your personal and professional goals and level up your life.

From here, you can add in your "hour of power" (if you have such a thing), your workouts, massages, and any other self-care routines you want.

I encourage you to identify at least one activity you can do each week that will completely relax and recharge you physically and mentally.

For example, my first online mentor, Ryan Lee, always took time off to get massages in the middle of the day. When he first told me about this I was a young personal trainer that thought you had to grind all day long, and that you might find time for such luxuries on the weekend. But Ryan was ahead of the peak performance game (this was 2002 after all), and it was these massage trips (plus his weekly afternoon trip to the movies) that actually helped him be more creative and productive.

That approach to life has inspired me and many of my clients to block time for the massage sessions, float tank visits, and other forms of recovery - even during the middle of a typical work day. As the old saying goes in airplane safety demonstrations, "You must put on your own oxygen mask before you can help others," we need to apply that same line of thinking to our minds and bodies each week.

Remember, I want you to start treating yourself like an elite athlete. If you were the head coach for a leading NBA team, would you train your star athlete to the point of exhaustion every single day? Of course not! You would *require* them to prioritize things like physical therapy, yoga, nutrition, chiropractor visits, and massages. Treat yourself the same way and realize that prioritizing self care isn't selfish or lazy, it's *necessary* for sustained success.

2. Schedule Your Peak Performance Routines

With your personal non-negotiables locked in, we're going to shift gears and schedule your "peak performance routines". To sustain the highest levels of performance and success, you must prioritize the habits and routines that give you clarity, reduce anxiety, and fuel success.

As such, the next thing you're going to put into your calendar is your Sunday and end of day planning and preparation. Block off thirty minutes on Sunday morning and fifteen minutes at the end of your work day where you will focus on reflection, planning, and preparation to ensure that each day goes as smoothly as possible.

Next, pull out your phone and make sure that you have a "Reverse Alarm" set for each day of the week and schedule your nighttime productivity routine. I also recommend that you set timers or calendar reminders to remind you to follow my 10-3-2-1-0 formula for incredible sleep.

With your reverse alarms set, you're now going to identify the "buffer time" you want to incorporate into your schedule. As a bare minimum, I suggest that you schedule at least three hours of buffer time once a week (an entire afternoon or morning) and two 30-minute blocks on other days throughout the week. If you have check-ins or calls with a coach or accountability partner, schedule those as well.

Now, with all of your self care, relationship, and peak performance rituals in place, you can shift your focus to crushing your big rocks.

3. Schedule Your Magic Time

Before scheduling any meetings, training calls, or other "Urgent Important" work, you're going to schedule your magic time. Earlier in this book, you used the "time journal" exercise to identify your magic time and now it's time to take that information and put it into your calendar.

For each of these blocks, I encourage you to write down *exactly* what you plan to do. What 'non urgent, important' (NUI) work are you committed to accomplishing? Will you write your book? Build a new product? Fix a sales funnel? Practice your presentation skills? Fix your finances?

What are the most important activities that, if completed every week, will drive you to your dream life the fastest? Next, I want you to think about how you can guard your magic time and prevent any interruptions from stunting your progress and focus?

What actionable steps are you going to take to "build a fence" around yourself and block out distractions? Will you put your phone on airplane mode? Unplug the router? Go to a coffee shop where your kids can't distract you? Get it out of your head and make a note of it on your grid or calendar.

Next, you're going to schedule something I call the "90-minute work day". This is where you're going to be sooooo productive that you literally accomplish as much work in one short block of time as you would on a regular day. This gives you a 20% boost in results and is one of the key factors in leaving your competition in the dust.

Years ago, while building my Turbulence Training online fitness business, I discovered that there was a secret "magic time" every week that allowed me to get 2-3X more accomplished than at any other time.

This secret slot is early Saturday morning. We've all experienced this. Maybe you woke up earlier than everyone else and snuck in a little bit of time on an important project. It felt so serene and spectacular because you got into the flow faster, and more importantly, you knew that no one would be bothering you on the phone or in your inbox. You tripled your productivity over any other time of week.

So why did you stop doing that? It's a secret to success.

Now don't worry, I'm not asking you to give up your weekends. All you need to do is devote 90 minutes on Saturday morning to getting ahead in life, and you'll make massive progress in whatever is important to you.

While the rest of the world is sleeping in, nursing a hangover, or cursing themselves for staying out so late the night before, you'll be building your empire faster than the competition. Fewer commitments and expectations allow you to tap into flow states more easily and go to an environment that elicits creativity (like a coffee shop or library) guilt free.

When I shared this strategy with my client Erin Wright, a 6-figure copywriter, she was able to crank out 2-3X more sales copy by spending 90-minutes at a coffee shop on a Saturday morning (while her family slept in at home) than any other day of the week.

I promise that if you commit to a Saturday morning secret magic time habit for the next 12-months, you will make the biggest leaps and bounds in your career. This is a game changer – ignore it at your own risk!

4. Schedule Work—and Everything Else

Finally, with everything else locked into your calendar, it's time to fill in the remainder of your work day.

By now, you've probably noticed that the sheer number of bumpers in your schedule make a 60+ hour work week all but impossible. With your relationship, self care, and magic time scheduled, you no longer have the time to attend pointless meetings, take useless calls, and go "for coffee" with everyone who reaches out to you.

Before you start filling in any of your remaining time blocks, I want you to review the Eisenhower Box and "Billionaire Time Matrix" you created earlier. Listen, you *know* what habits, activities, and obligations aren't serving you and it's your responsibility to eradicate them from your schedule and stick to your commitment to what matters.

By doing so, you will create more freedom in your life and make available more mental, physical, and emotional energy for what really matters in life (such as your family, fitness, faith, finances, and your big goals and dreams).

This might require you to take two steps back in the short term (i.e. sacrificing today's profits so that you can hire and train a new employee to double tomorrow's profits), but I promise you, if you implement the lessons I've been teaching you, you'll take a quantum leap toward your dream life in the long term).

Fill in whatever tasks remain and as you do, keep asking yourself, "Does this *need* to be done and if so, does it need to be done by me?" If the answer is "no", then eliminate it from your schedule or delegate to someone else. Your Perfect Days, Weeks, and Life depend on it.

Customizing Your Perfect Calendar

Although the foundational principles on which this formula is built are immutable--e.g. Building your business around your life, prioritizing relationships, taking care of you first, etc.--the exact application of these principles is malleable.

You don't *have* to work on "normal" work days (i.e. Friday). You don't *have* to schedule date night on a workday. You don't *have* to go to Grandma's for dinner on Sunday. As long as you follow the overarching principles of this formula, you can customize the Perfect Week Formula to whatever precise schedule you desire.

For example, my client Blair Cornel runs a booming financial advisory firm. When he first started working with me, his goal was to take a long weekend *every* weekend. That meant when he got home Thursday night, it was family-time only until he showed back up at the office on Monday morning.

If you think this is impossible, check this out. Within three weeks Blair and I had customized his perfect week so that he could take his first Friday off. Now that meant making sacrifices. He was forced to cut out family time on Tuesday and Thursday nights so he could meet clients in the office until 8 pm, but the plan worked. Within 90 days he was on a full-time four-day work week, and quickly realized that he would rather work 40 hours in 4 days and enjoy a weekly three day weekend than work fewer hours over more days.

Another example is my co-author Austin Gillis. He crams in all of his weekly conference calls every Monday afternoon. Since he isn't able to fully relax until these calls are complete, he works Thursday to Monday and takes Tuesdays and Wednesdays as his weekend.

And that's the beauty of this formula. You can make it fit whatever schedule you want to have and your days don't have to be the same.

You can make this formula work for *you* without feeling like you have to adhere to arbitrary rules or routines. You can customize, personalize, and mold it however you like so that you can experience *your* Perfect Weeks every week for the rest of your life.

Do This Now

Now, it's time to plan your very first Perfect Week and make the world play by your Rules.

Take everything that you've learned from this book and create your first 7X7 "Perfect Week Grid" using the worksheet provided on the next page. Commit to this planning structure for at least one month and enlist the help of a coach or accountability partner to make this stick.

During the first few weeks, you should expect to experience some resistance and feel like you are taking a step backwards. It's ok. These growing pains are a normal part of the process. Trust that this system works. It's worked for my millionaire clients (and my beginner entrepreneur clients and busy mom and dad readers too) and it will work for you.

If you commit to putting this calendar into practice week after week and month after month, you can and will experience the most productive and fulfilling weeks of your life more consistently than you ever have before.

PERFECT WEEK FORMULA

	Monday	Tuesday	Wednesday	Thursday	Friday	Saturday	Sunday
m							
m							
m							
m							
m							
m							
m							

Take action on this formula *this* week and be sure to send your feedback and success stories to support@earlytorise. com We read every email and I can't *wait* to hear how the Perfect Week Formula changes your life.

YOUR PERFECT LIFE AWAITS

Before you close the book and take what you've learned and implement it into your life and business, I first want to say, "Congratulations."

If you've read this far, you have taken a big step toward building a life on your terms and achieving the freedom you've been after for so many years.

But this is only the beginning.

To build your business around your life and have the family, health, wealth, happiness, *and* success you desire, you must commit to taking consistent daily action and trust the process.

I've already highlighted dozens of client success stories throughout this book and shared how *The Perfect Week Formula* has equipped high-performers just like you with the systems and structure they needed to breakthrough to the next level of success in their lives and businesses.

This system *works*.

And no matter how chaotic, crazy, and stressful your life might be today, you make a change.

Just like my buddy Bedros who I introduced you to in the introduction.

When I started coaching Bedros, his life was chaotic, unpredictable, and overwhelming – and most of that was *his* fault. He admits to procrastinating during the day which led to cramming in work late at night. That led to overeating, missing workouts, and a descent into chaos that nearly cost him everything.

He never had time for the things that mattered most, his anxiety was out of control, his business was flat lining, and every day was a struggle.

But like every Hero's Journey, Bedros found the mentor (me) to guide him from his lowest lows back onto a path where he could go and achieve his highest highs. Today, he has it all. There's not a man I know who has it more together.

He leads one of the fastest growing fitness franchises on the planet with more than 800 locations worldwide and 9-figures in yearly revenue. He speaks at stadiums packed with tens of thousands of people, travels regularly with his wife and kids, and holds business seminars for American military veterans. He also teams up with me in his spare time to co-host the top rated Empire Podcast Show, and run the Empire Mastermind – a coaching group for high performing entrepreneurs like you.

But even more important than his impressive professional accomplishments is the way that Bedros shows up to life *outside* of his professional pursuits.

Despite the demands and challenges of his businesses and constantly growing team, Bedros has strategically engineered his life to make time for the things that matter most.

He takes his wife and daughter on weekly date nights (separately, of course!), is in the best shape of his life with visible abs at 44, and still finds the time to play the drums with his son, do regular 6-week challenges to support his personal growth, and to crush every single friend and colleague who challenges his ping pong abilities (seriously... the man is a ping pong *machine*).

Today, Bedros still hires me to coach him and his team every year and he *still* works to refine his strategies and get even more out of himself, his business, and his life.

His transformation didn't happen overnight. But his consistency and commitment allowed him to overcome his biggest obstacles and build the life of his dreams.

And the craziest part?

Bedros isn't special (just don't tell him I said that...).

Just like all of my other millionaire clients, he's just a regular, good person who made the *decision* to take uncommon action. He does things that others won't so that he can live the life that others can't.

And no matter where you are today, man or woman, single or married, young or old, beginner or already successful entrepreneur, you can use the systems and strategies I've shared with you to create more balance, structure, and success in every area of your life.

This system works... and has worked from readers aged 18 to 82, and it will work for you too – IF *you* take a positive attitude and commit to making it work.

Attitude is critical. Two people in practically the same situation in life can interpret advice in extremely different ways.

Case in point. For my first book, The Perfect Day Formula, my most critical 3-star review was from a mom of one who said, "Oh, this won't work for me, it's impossible."

I have to admit, that stung. Until, that is, I read the most popular positive review from a mother of *three* who said, "This book is exactly what I've been waiting for! If you commit to the program, it will change your life!"

High performers in life have a can-do attitude, while those who refuse to open their mind to a new way of thinking are condemned to eternal "struckle."

But remember, what got you *here* won't get you *there*.

To build a life and business on your terms and enjoy the freedom, impact, and income you desire, you must do things differently than you've done before.

You must be willing to think and act in a way that is uncommon and, for many of you, uncomfortable.

The path in front of you will not be easy. You will be tempted to quit and go back to your old way of doing things.

Don't.

Trust the process. Put in the work. And I promise you, your life will never be the same.

I know you're capable of so much more and you believe it in your heart. Time to put the pen to paper, do the work, formulate your Perfect Weeks, and live your Perfect Life.

To Your Success!

Sincerely,

Craig Ballantyne
Craig@PerfectWeekFormula.com

QUICK REMINDER!

To get the most out of *The Perfect Week Formula* system, be sure to go to https://PerfectWeekFormula.com/sheets to download your free printable copy of the Eisenhower Matrix, Billionaire Time Matrix, Time Journal, and 7X7 Grid.

ABOUT CRAIG BALLANTYNE

Craig Ballantyne is the author of *The Perfect Day Formula,
The Perfect Week Formula,* and the Wall Street Journal best-
seller *Unstoppable.* As an international coach and business
strategist, Craig is most widely known for his inhuman
discipline and proven systems that help top-performing
entrepreneurs increase their performance and double their
revenue...while working less.

His raw, no-nonsense coaching style and actionable
strategies have empowered clients like Joe Polish, Shanda
Sumpter, Sharran Srivatsaa, Joel Marion, Jason Capital, and
Bedros Keuilian to build the lives of their dreams... making
"Empire Money" while working far less than the average
business owner.

The people who work with Craig are driven. Relentless. And, often, gifted with more potential than they realize.

If this sounds like you, we invite you to explore working with Craig and can confidently say that his methods will not only CHANGE your life... They'll completely TRANSFORM IT. You'll increase your impact, your influence, AND income... and finally achieve true work-life balance.

To learn more about how Craig can help you scale your business, work less, and develop the systems and discipline you need to succeed in every area of life, just email Craig@ PerfectWeekFormula.com or contact me on Instagram @ RealCraigBallantyne